THANKSGIVING RECIPES

A Classic Thanksgiving Cookbook

(Enjoy the Divine Taste of Thanksgiving With These 50+ Delicious Recipes)

Matthew Fargo

Published by Alex Howard

© **Matthew Fargo**

All Rights Reserved

Thanksgiving Recipes: A Classic Thanksgiving Cookbook (Enjoy the Divine Taste of Thanksgiving With These 50+ Delicious Recipes)

ISBN 978-1-989891-93-3

All rights reserved. No part of this guide may be reproduced in any form without permission in writing from the publisher except in the case of brief quotations embodied in critical articles or reviews.

Legal & Disclaimer

The information contained in this book is not designed to replace or take the place of any form of medicine or professional medical advice. The information in this book has been provided for educational and entertainment purposes only.

The information contained in this book has been compiled from sources deemed reliable, and it is accurate to the best of the Author's knowledge; however, the Author cannot guarantee its accuracy and validity and cannot be held liable for any errors or omissions. Changes are periodically made to this book. You must consult your doctor or get professional medical advice before using any of the suggested remedies, techniques, or information in this book.

Table of contents

Part 1 1
Introduction 2
Chapter 1: Avoiding Thanksgiving Stress 7
Chapter 2: Getting Organized For Your Thanksgiving Celebration At Home 13
Chapter 3: Planning The Family Thanksgiving Meal 27
Chapter 4: Decorating For Thanksgiving 45
Chapter 5: Setting The Table For Thanksgiving 63
Chapter 6: Planning The Perfect Thanksgiving Party 72
Chapter 7: Thanksgiving Activities 77
Chapter 8: A Traditional Thanksgiving Menu 87
1-Traditional Roast Turkey With Chestnut Stuffing And Homemade Gravy 88
Preparing the Chestnut Stuffing 89
2-Roast Turkey 91
3-Roast Turkey Breast 95
4-Turkey Gravy 97
5-Homemade Cornbread 100
7-Classic Shrimp Cocktail 104
8-Apple, Onion and Squash Tart 107
9-Stuffed Portobello Mushrooms 109
10-Roasted Beet, Orange and Onion Salad 111
11-Butternut Squash Soup 114
12-Classic Cream of Mushroom Soup 116
13-Classic Green Bean Casserole 119
14-Homemade French Fried Onions 120

15-Creamy Thanksgiving Mashed Potatoes................ 122
Candied Yams 124
17-Roasted Root Vegetables... 127
18-Rice Pilaf with Wild Rice 129
19-Down Home Flaky Biscuits 131
20-Traditional Cranberry Sauce................................... 133
21-Cranberry Pumpkin Bread 134
22-Pumpkin Pecan Muffins... 136
23-All Butter Pie Crust 138
24-Easy Pumpkin Pie 140
25-Homemade Creamy Whipped Topping................. 142
26-Fancy Lattice Apple Pie... 143
27-No-Bake Cranberry Crisp Cookie Squares............ 146
28-Spiced Oatmeal and Pear Cookies........................ 148
29-Sparkling Cranberry Punch 150
30-Mulled Apple Cider 151
Chapter 9: The Thanksgiving Holiday Does Not Mean You Have To Gain Weight....................................... 153
Chapter 10: Organizing Your Leftovers 156
Conclusion.. 163
Part 2... 164
Introduction 165
Appetizers 167
Thanks For Cheese 'N Artichoke Dip.......................... 167
Smoked Salmon With Dill And Cheese 168
Tomato Caprese Whimsy 170
Bacon-Wrapped Dates.. 171

Tomato Pancetta-Stuffed Mushrooms 173
Bell Pepper Hummus 175
Bacon Chips 176
Spicy Shrimp Appies 178
Zucchini Fritter 179
Cheesy Spinach-Stuffed Crepes 181
Spiced Almond Nut Butter Dip 183
Sides 184
Garlicky Swiss Chard 184
Asparagus With Creamy Béchamel .... **Error! Bookmark not defined.**
Spinach And Feta Salad .... **Error! Bookmark not defined.**
Fall Veggie Fries .... **Error! Bookmark not defined.**
Spicy Eggplant .... **Error! Bookmark not defined.**
How To Carve A Turkey 186
How To Set 187
A Table 187

Part 1

Introduction

Thanksgiving in the United States is supposed to be a family-oriented holiday in which we get time off work to spend with family and friends. It coincides to a certain extent with harvest time in North America, so the special meal we serve at Thanksgiving is in part a celebration of the bounty of nature. The Thanksgiving meal is also meant to reflect the meal the Pilgrims shared with the indigenous people they began to live near when European settlers crossed the Atlantic and began to establish colonies in the New World. No, the Pilgrims did not have mashed potatoes and green bean casserole at their celebration. They might not even have eaten turkey. The two descriptions of the feast which took place in the early autumn, not November, mentions 'wildfowl' that they shot, and 5 deer for venison that the Native Americans brought with them, and mentions in passing a lot of wild turkeys in the area. Even if they had turkey, it would have been boiled, not roasted, which was their method of cooking smaller birds. Over the passage of time, popular dishes from Pilgrim times have faded into the background and been replaced with bread stuffing, turkey, and so on, until at this point, these dishes have become an almost inescapable part of the traditional Thanksgiving meal in America.

Those setting up their own home for the first time, especially if they have a new young family, can easily become overwhelmed at all the pressure that surrounds the Thanksgiving holiday. If you are not much of a cook, it can seem very intimidating, especially because these days, the Thanksgiving meal seems to be more important than anything other part of this holiday. The only thing that might seem more important to some households is the shopping the next day, Black Friday, as it is called, when the Christmas and end of year shopping season gets into full For those who want to observe a more traditional Thanksgiving, with the emphasis on Thanks, it can seem as if they are out of step with the rest of the world piling food on their plates as they shout at the football on the TV.
It is your home, your holiday, and your family values, so in this guide we will be offering a range of suggestions that will cater to a range of tastes and personal preferences. In particular, we will be offering easy to make and inexpensive recipes for your Thanksgiving feast, even if you have never hosted in your home before.

Cooking has become a bit of a lost art in these days of takeaways and food ordering apps on your mobile phone, but cooking yourself is the best way to save money and eat well for a fraction of the cost of prepared foods and restaurant meals. We were both fortunate enough to have grandparents and parents who were interested in cooking when we were growing up, and were of a generation that did not have microwaves. We learned how to cook from scratch from all of our relatives. Over the years Evelyn has been working in health publishing, she has mastered not only traditional cooking, but vegetarian and vegan cooking for herself and certain members of her family. Mara has always enjoyed cooking as a hobby and tried to master American regional cooking, including Cajun and Creole.

Mara also loved making arts and crafts projects, teaching herself sewing, knitting, and other functional crafts. Once she became a mother, it was even more fun to come up with ideas

to keep the little ones busy.
The holidays are supposed to be an opportunity to spend quality time with your family, not exhaust yourself, overspend and overeat. This guide is intended for beginner cooks and busy parents who want to live better for less, stretching their budget as far as it can go with filling and delicious fool-proof recipes their family and guests will love without spending hours slaving in the kitchen.

This guide is also designed to help you make the most of your time off work and keep the all your guests and any children you may have entertained before, during and after the holiday. In particular, it will be important to keep the children busy because they will be out of school and need to be kept occupied so they do not get into mischief. Having them help with the holiday preparation, planning and decoration are the best ways to accomplish this and still have fun as a family.

If you are a single person hosting a gathering of friends, this guide will help you plan a sit down meal or a Thanksgiving party with a range of traditional recipes that will impress all your guests. You will learn how to organize your event and any contributions your visitors will be making to the festivities, so there are no gaps in the meal.

If you are like Evelyn and live in a large city, there will always be people spending the holiday on their own because their families are too far away. Those new to this country as well might not understand what all the fuss is all about, while others really love seeing a real traditional American holiday like Thanksgiving. It is a novelty for them because they do not usually have anything similar in their own country. How great would it be to become such a confident Thanksgiving cook that you would feel able to invite anyone over so they are not alone for the holiday?

In this guide, you will also learn how to handle leftovers from the meal so that nothing goes to waste and you can save money by making the most of seasonal foods and the time you spend cooking on the day.

Any readers familiar with Mara's series of <u>Make and Freeze meals</u> recipe guides knows that making your own TV style dinners, or cooking in advance and freezing the leftovers, or cooking in bulk with a view to making extra meals to stock the freezer, is a great way to cook for a number of reasons.

Pound for pound, you will save a great deal of money compared to buying TV dinners and other convenience foods in the store. Your leftovers will never go to waste again, lost in the shuffle or shoved to the back of the fridge until they are too old to eat safely.

If you are a busy mom on the go, make and freeze meals mean you never have to worry again about what your family is eating if you are not there to supervise. If you are a busy single person, cook once, portion out 4 or 5 meals, and cruise through the rest of the month with a freeze full of food.

Family person or single, you can also use your freezer to help you cook ahead for the holidays, making Thanksgiving stress-free because you will have prepared things ahead of time that just need to be defrosted and/or reheated.

Thanksgiving might be only for your immediate family at home, or you might be expecting your entire extended family to descend upon you like a horde of locusts. You might have a community gathering, with friends, neighbors and so on also joining you at your holiday table. You might also be joining others at their home and looking for ideas for easy recipes you can make and bring as your contribution to the festivities.

Bringing your own contribution is a generous gesture, of course, but it is also an essential holiday survival strategy if you wish to avoid packing on the pounds, or have a special eating lifestyle that might cause you to be concerned that you might not be able to find something to eat when you go to a meal outside your home.

For example, there are many vegetarians and vegans. Food allergies are more common than ever, such as egg and nut allergies. Many people are adopting a gluten-free lifestyle. Or you might be counting calories or following a low carb diet to slim down, or to try to stay slim despite all of the seasonal temptations surrounding you.

Mara has already produced a guide on Low Carb Recipes for Thanksgiving if you are watching your weight, sticking to a low carb diet, or want to go gluten free because you have allergies or sensitivities. Note that even though those recipes are low carb, they are also not too high in calories either, and are not full of weird or expensive ingredients.

In guide you are reading now, you will find a full menu of traditional recipes for the Thanksgiving meal itself, and for some of the leftover turkey, to make ahead and freeze, or to help feed the whole family cheaply while everyone is home from work or school for the long weekend.

Holidays are supposed to be special, not stressful. They are certainly an exciting time for children. In this guide, you will also discover a range of ways to channel that energy into fun decorating projects, activities, and more, for children of all ages.

Let's start with the essentials, avoiding stress at Thanksgiving, and then move on to planning your meal, and getting the house ready with delightful decorations.

Chapter 1: Avoiding Thanksgiving Stress

Are you getting stressed just thinking about the holiday season approaching? Given how hard we all work these days just to earn a paycheck, that is not surprising.

But there are many other reasons too why Thanksgiving may give us the jitters. From the stress caused by having to plan a multiple-course meal for many people, to being questioned again by your aunt as to why you aren't as successful as Cousin Chris, or why you've gained 10 pounds, the holidays can be more of a trial than tremendous fun. Especially if you are hosting this year.

Fortunately, there are a lot of things you can do to reduce this kind of holiday stress, so that you can have fun too and not end up completely exhausted.

The first way to relieve stress is to re-gain control. It is YOUR holiday. You are in charge. These are your days off. It is up to you how you choose to spend them. Reminding yourself of these essential facts can empower you to take charge without being seen as pushy, uncooperative, or a party pooper.

We should all do what we feel most comfortable with, according to our abilities, and yes, our financial means as well. It is pointless to feel pressured into hosting a large gathering and go into debt to do so, since this will only add up to even more stress on what should be a joyful occasion.

If you and your family and friends have celebrated Halloween recently, you might be feeling rather tired of all sorts of goodies and treats. If Christmas is a huge deal in your family, perhaps a more modest celebration at Thanksgiving would be a good strategy.

On the other hand, if you do not observe either Halloween or Christmas in a big way, Thanksgiving might be your favorite holiday, and one that you love to go all out on. Even when Evelyn lived overseas, she would do her best to put together a full Thanksgiving feast. She fondly remembers the emergency phone calls from her mother each year on exactly how to cook the sweet potato casserole, an essential family favorite. One of the reasons why she became a cookbook writer in her spare time was because so few of her friends cooked, and how often they asked how to make even the most basic dishes.

If this is the first Thanksgiving you will ever be hosting in your own home as an adult, congratulations and welcome. We promise that even you can succeed in creating a great meal if you plan ahead and follow the recipes as exactly as written.

We will be giving you a range of worksheets and other downloads to help you with all of your chores, shopping and cooking. Think of it as a stress-free Thanksgiving in a box. Download all your worksheets into one folder in your computer, make copies of them, and you will be able to use them over and over again year after year.

As you start to stress about Thanksgiving, remember that it is your budget in terms of time and money. If you are stuck working long hours every day, you will have a lot less time to plan and prepare a fabulous feast as compared with, say, your aunt, who is retired and perky enough to go golfing every day, but sits at your house wanting to be waited on hand and foot.

If you have to work on the Friday after Thanksgiving, that will also influence the amount of time you want to spend preparing your Thanksgiving decorations and meals, and when and for how long the guests will be visiting. Not everyone is fortunate enough to get that day off. Even if they do, they might have plans for it as well. If you are a couple, for instance, you might make both sets of parents happy by visiting one on the Thursday and the other on the Friday, or even the Saturday or Sunday, if they live nearby.

In Evelyn's home, depending on our work schedules and wider family plans, we might not actually celebrate with the full meal and all the trimmings until the Saturday. Or sometimes we get roped into both, Thanksgiving with one set of parents at their place, and the second set of parents at our own home.

For Mara, the family usually comes to her, but she has a set group of helpers who contribute certain parts of the meal each year. Mara's children are still quite young, so that places a burden on her and hubby to keep the children busy while they are out of school so they do not get too bored and start acting up.

Evelyn's children are young teens now, but she often has new foster children, plus emergency foster dogs at this time of year. The children and hubby are a big help, however, so she is blessed enough to know that she can be confident that there will always be good food on the table or in the fridge or freezer for anyone who shows up at the holidays, no matter how busy she is with publishing deadlines. Since she is also vegetarian, she has meals suitable for any eating lifestyle on hand at all times. This then makes it easier if she is invited out, since she can easily bring a dish she is sure she and the family can eat, and which others might enjoy as well.

Not everyone likes turkey, of course, but the side dishes are usually pretty yummy in their own right, and many can be made vegetarian or even vegan if you use vegetable stock, soy margarine, soy cheese and egg substitute in your recipes, and some form or non-dairy milk or cream such as soy, almond or rice milk. These can be expensive alternatives, however, so in our recipes we try to stick to the basics as much as possible in terms of ingredients you will use regularly, not use once for the holidays and then shove to the back of the shelf.

Take into account your own stress factors when planning your celebration this year. Look at them honestly, and do not try to minimize them. If you do, you will end up struggling, or worse still, feel resentful that you have to do it all while everyone else is sitting around in front of the TV digesting and the kids are wrecking the place because they haven't been outside all day. This can easily happen if the weather is very cold and wet.

For example, Evelyn was once given a huge assignment to complete by the Monday after Thanksgiving in one job with a particularly difficult boss. She explained to the family and to help keep down her stress, they took care of all the shopping and preparation work according to her notes she had kept in her worksheet folder from the previous year. All she would have to do was cook the turkey on the day. The rest got warmed in the oven or microwave.

With all of the help she got, she was able to complete the assignment a week early, and was able to test all of the pages until the Wednesday with the help of her colleagues, so the entire new marketing site was completely ready by the time she left on the Wednesday evening.

And a good thing too, because at 9AM on the Monday morning, the boss called her into the office and demanded to know where the website was. She was able to proudly show him that it was 100% up and running. "Oh, but you can't possibly have tested it yet!" he sneered. She told him that all of the staff had, but he was free to send her a list of anything he might find that was broken. She knew he was just looking for an excuse to fire her so he could bring his own friends into the company, a stressful enough situation at the best of times.

She knew he believed she would have been stressed and overloaded due to the holidays, and that most people would have come in the first thing after Thanksgiving with some sort of excuse or new timetable. Teamwork meant everything got done in the end and everyone succeeded in their goals, including work goals and life goals, having time to spend with the people who are important in your life.

We are sharing this example with you to demonstrate that we all need help from time to time, and teamwork can take the stress out of even the most difficult situations. This story also demonstrates that not every single year has to be exactly the same. But keeping all of your worksheets, menu plans and so on can help you every year, so you do not have to start from scratch each time to plan your Thanksgiving gathering.

By planning a whole schedule for the month, Thanksgiving Day, and Thanksgiving weekend, you can stress less because you will be sure nothing has been forgotten. Plan your Turkey Timetable, everyone can have fun, eat well, and be entertained. All of the cooking, cleaning before and after, and left overs, will all be take care of without any one single person being overly burdened and stressed out.

Sounds good? Then let's get started. We are going to cover the essentials that you can plan ahead for, so that you can work in your holiday preparations with your regular daily life, chores, and to do lists. A little extra each day will mean you do not feel so overwhelmed on the day itself. We will begin with getting organized.

Chapter 2: Getting Organized For Your Thanksgiving Celebration At Home

Your first step in tackling Thanksgiving is to get organized. In the resources section of this guide, you will find a range of worksheets and planners to help you with this. Download them first, and then come back to this page.

Once you have downloaded them, we suggest you create a Thanksgiving folder on your computer to store them. Then we suggest you create a folder for your current year, 2014, 2015 and so on. Copy a full set of the worksheets into the folder. In this way, in case you make any mistakes, you still have the original you can make a copy of.

Store everything related to Thanksgiving this year in the digital folder to help keep everything organized as you work your way through this guide. You might also wish to create a paper folder to have on hand to put your jottings, notes, copies of recipes, lists, clippings and so on into.

In this way, you can not only plan for a successful, stress-free

Thanksgiving this year, you will also have all your files and notes to refer to again next year, and for many years to come, which will make your job even easier in the future. Shopping lists, decorations you already have stored, versus ones you might need to buy or make, can all be saved on your computer or in your paper folder and referred to as you work your way through your to do list.

We use reliable back up storage in the cloud and Google documents as well to store really important items that we do not wish to lose if anything goes wrong with our computer. With <u>Google docs</u>, you can not only store the items safely, you can also access them from any computer you are using once you log in. You can also invite people to share the document/s, so you can all be on the same page when it comes to holiday planning.

Another fun, and very visual way to organize yourself, is to create a virtual pinboard on Pinterest. You can also invite others to pin on your board. It will be visible to others, of course, so do not pin anything you would be worried about other people seeing. You could create a Thanksgiving decorations board, a menu board, activities, and more.

But even with back up and good storage, it is possible to lose data. We recommend that you organize and save your favorite recipes for Thanksgiving all in one place for each special holiday so you do not need to hunt for them each year. There is nothing worse than reaching for a particular cookbook on your shelf only to find that someone has borrowed it and not given it back.

Even worse is when you had a favorite website or blog you used over and over, only to discover that the site has shut down, or undergone such an extensive reorganization that all the URLs have changed.

Recipes

In reference to recipes from books, we scan in our favorite recipes, or photocopy them, and put the copies in our digital and paper folders. In this way we avoid soiling our cookbooks while cooking. On the paper copies, we use sticky notes to make notes and adjustments to each recipe once we have cooked it through at least once to see how the chef intended it to come out. With the paper copy in front of us, we do not need to worry about finding an Internet connection or our wireless hub being down.

We can also make notes on the digital copies, and best of all, email them to anyone who asks for a copy.

The photocopies also make it easier to pass along the recipe to anyone who asks for it. We will always print out some to bring some along if we go to a community gathering such as a potluck, so people will know exactly what they are eating and can grab a copy of the recipe easily if they really like it.

We like to keep one master copy of the recipe in a <u>plastic sheet protector</u> so it will stay relatively clean and stainifree no matter how many times it is handled. It can be wiped if it gets spattered, and we can stand it up easily in a book rack or even tape or stick it to a wall or counter without the page getting torn over time.

On the computer, we can copy and paste the recipes for future reference. By keeping them in the Thanksgiving folder, it is easy to find them and forward them to anyone who wants a copy.

The paper copies and digital copies are also handy so people will know exactly what is in the dish/es you have prepared. With so many people with nut allergies, egg allergies, gluten sensitivities and so on, either they might need to be warned about certain ingredients, or you might wish to cook recipes with no known allergens in them in order to try to keep everyone safe.

For example, these days, if we have a recipe that calls for nuts, we suggest other alternatives that will still allow the dish to come out well and for everyone to stay safe. Mara's children are not allergic, but many of their school friends are, so better safe than sorry.

Those on special diets, such as vegetarian, vegan, or gluten-free, will appreciate the effort you make by keeping them in mind, and using only suitable and safe ingredients for them.

If you are bringing a contribution to a potluck or a family meal at someone else's home, the last thing you want to do is make others sick, or put them at risk. Preparing a dish with no known allergens is the ideal way to do this. Yes, it is your holiday too, but we want everyone to enjoy it. You can eat whatever you like in your own house when it is just your family, but in the wider community, it always pays to cater in such a way that you can be sure everyone stays safe.

If you have any food issues yourself, then bring one or more dishes with you to share that you can be sure you will be able to eat, and share with others. Evelyn has been a vegetarian for many years now, and has expanded other people's horizons through the dishes she has brought with her to various functions, which are tasty enough to satisfy even the most raging carnivore.

If you keep everything in one place, like a master notebook, spreadsheet or folder for Thanksgiving, it will help you juggle everything more successfully. And don't forget them just because the holiday is over. Make notes on them as you get feedback from your guests, and then you can update them on the computer.

Guest Lists

Just as important as your recipes are your guest lists. You can't make any final meal plans without first deciding how many people you are going to invite, who they are bringing, what their special dietary needs are, if any. Mara can remember her brothers bringing home a new girlfriend each at the last minute almost every year, and having to cater to a range of needs.

One or two dishes suited for vegans that have no nuts or gluten in them might sound tough, but it can be done if you plan ahead. In this way, you will be sure to have something nice to eat no matter who shows up.

The second key reason to organize your guest list early is in order to delegate. Since our goal is to have a stress-free Thanksgiving, remember that you are not Super Person and will need help before, during and after the meal. Delegating mean you can have a good time too without slaving over a hot stove and feeling unappreciated.

The third reason is to organize contributions to the meal. Feeding a family of 5 or 7 for Thanksgiving is tough enough these days, take our word for it, without adding extra mouths and needing to cater for 12, 20, even 40 people, as Evelyn often does for the end of year holidays.

When issuing your invitations, either ask for an item specifically, or give suggested categories. This should ensure that you end up with a well-rounded meal with a range of typical side dishes to go with your turkey, not one green bean casserole and 20 pumpkin pies.

As they RSVP, get a firm undertaking as to what they are going to bring. Write it down on your guest list next to any special food needs they might have. With everyone chipping in one dish or item, your gathering will quickly turn into a large and fabulous meal, with no one feeling overly stressed or burdened.

Or, if you are concerned about food allergies in the household and do not want any food to go to waste, or people to get sick, or you have family members and friends who are "culinarily challenged", ask them to contribute other items, such as chips, beverages, napkins, paper plates and so on.

Chores

Don't be shy to ask your family and friends to help clean and get ready for the big day. They can run errands for you, help set the table, decorate and cook with you. They can also help keep an eye on the children. As long as they aren't the interfering "I'm always right" even when you know they are wrong types, you should be fine.

We all talk about spring cleaning, but every season is a good opportunity for a thorough going over in each room, and a way to keep down clutter. Your first chore before anything else will usually be cleaning, so you can then decorate. As you cook, your cleaning will be ongoing. Using items like foil, cooking parchment, or <u>Silpat</u> can all help with quick and easy clean ups so you do not need to spend hours scrubbing pots and pans. Paper plates can cut down on the amount of washing up that needs to be done, but they can be expensive, and some plates very flimsy. Plastic cutlery can be re-used, but most people throw it away, which can be expensive and wasteful. Again, do what makes sense for your time budget and financial budget, and recycle whenever possible.

Anyone who does not help with the preparation before the meal can always help with the clean up afterwards, even if it is just clearing the table between courses and ferrying plates to the kitchen. Most people can also handle scraping them down and washing them. We keep some plastic aprons in festive holiday colors like orange, green and yellow for helpers to slip on so they do not get their nice clothes dirty. Turkey can be rather greasy, after all.

While it is true that you are hosting and it is your home, but you don't have to handle everything on your own. If you try, and end up feeling frazzled and unappreciated, your guests will feel uncomfortable and won't enjoy the day as much. If you are juggling work as well as home commitments, it can seem like military maneuvers to get ready for Thanksgiving. You do not want to end up even more exhausted than before you got your days off from work.

If you are a freelancer, this might actually be the worst time of year for you to take a few days off because you need steady income. If you are business owner, taking time off can be tough because you are already in the middle of trying to have a successful end of year selling season. Do delegate, and do not be a perfectionist.

And yes, we will be providing a range of recipes you can make from scratch at the end of this guide, but if you just do not have the time, it is fine to take short-cuts to relieve your stress. No, it is true there is nothing quite like homemade, but it is perfectly fine to use pop and fresh rolls, pre-made cranberry sauce in a can or jar, or frozen pies that you will bake in the oven once the turkey comes out of it. Again, stress free is being realistic about you can and can't do, afford, or have time for, not about 'being perfect'.

There is another reason to take short cuts if you have to. While we might be good cooks in some areas, we might not do so well with others. For example, Evelyn excels at main meals, vegetarian, and ethnic cuisines from around the world, but her cakes and desserts are not nearly as spectacular as Mara's.

Mara learned baking from her grandmother, and regional American cooking from a variety of courses she has attended, including Cajun and Creole cooking down in New Orleans. If you delegate any cooking to any family members, play to their strengths to make up for any weaknesses you might have.

Some Thanksgiving recipes have a traditional New England feel, since the first Thanksgiving was celebrated in the Massachusetts colony, but over the years, the traditional recipes have been added to and often given a Southern-style twist, such as pecans in the stuffing, pies, or even cranberry sauce.

You might wish to organize your recipes around a theme. It might also be interesting to see if any of you guests have regional dishes that are traditional in their family that they could bring for everyone to try.

Of course, delegating to friends and family assumes you have a cooperative group of people coming to your Thanksgiving celebration. But what if that isn't quite the case?

Coping with the Relatives and even your own family and friends

We have a lot of different people in our family, but you probably recognize the more difficult ones: control freaks, know it alls, the lazy ones who sit on their butts and want to be waited on hand and foot, and the nosy ones. Most of the time, we probably avoid them, but at the holidays, this may be impossible.

But remember, this is your celebration, so you call the shots.

Don't be afraid to delegate tasks, dishes to donate, and chores to perform. Have aprons and rubber gloves on hand so they can't have any excuse to duck out of the work, unless they are really not able-bodied.

But if a person can't do anything other than sit down, there is a lot they can do to help. Peeling potatoes, cleaning shrimp, shelling peas or tipping and topping green beans are all things even men can do, and can even do in front of the TV!

For the control freaks and know alls, let them work out their perfectionism by setting the table, or helping with the coats when the guests arrive, or the dishes and other items that the guests will be bringing. Just don't let them cook in the same kitchen with you. Evelyn's meals are usually for around 40 people, but all the women in the family know to just stand back and let her get on with it. They help with the serving, and the men with the cleaning up afterwards.

As for the nosy ones, you can pretty much predict the kind of embarrassing personal questions they are going to ask, so be prepared with a couple of polite replies and do not let them stress you.

Practice in the mirror how you'll answer those questions if you need to. If you know you'll get questions about weight gain or your husband's lost job', decide the best way to handle it without being rude.

If you still feel uneasy about the event, have a family member or two in the know to help run interference to keep the busybody occupied while you get on with your stress-free entertaining. You might even arrange a secret signal between you and your helper so they will know to come rescue you.

Or better still, get these nosy people to talk about themselves. Most people love that anyway!

One other issue to consider when you are organizing your guest list, menu, recipes, shopping and chores list is if anyone will be staying with you during the holiday. Having houseguests will add to the preparation as you get their accommodation ready. This scenario will require some thought and menu planning in advance to be sure you are able to feed them all the meals they will need while they are visiting.

You will have to plan for breakfast, lunch, dinner, and snacks for each day they will be with you, and then the big meal on Thanksgiving Day. You will also need to plan some sort of activities so they will not be bored during their stay with you. A timetable of events with the most important ones penciled in can help their visit go more smoothly and still give you the chance to do what is most important to you.

For example, if you always go to church on Thanksgiving, and on Sunday, note that down, but do not force them to go with you. Explain that they are more than welcome to come, but if they do not wish to, that can be their free time and you will all meet up at X for brunch, lunch and so on.

Decorating

Most of us will decorate our homes long before the guests arrive, but some wait until the day in order to get a range of contributions from the guests. This helps keep them occupied so they do not get bored. It also helps them feel like they are participating in the holiday more fully.

We like to organize our decorations around the house, but give the children and adults a craft table in an undecorated part of the room. We organize a range of art supplies and keep poster putty at the ready. They can make a range of decorations and put them on the walls. They can also create additional ones and bring them home as party favors.

Some projects are super simple; all you need are the raw materials. In other case, you might need to print out worksheets, games, and other printables. Store them in file folders, and the raw materials in a box or storage bin you can take out and put away any time you need to. Then you will see how easy and stress free decorating can be.

Shopping   Lists

Once you have organized all of the other lists, you can start to finalize your shopping lists. In terms of decorations and non-perishable items, you can buy them three months or so in advance, which will spread the cost of the holiday, and perhaps even Halloween and Thanksgiving, over the course of several months, not just one at a time. For example, gold paper plates, napkins and so on, with the gold more on the brown than the white end of the spectrum, can be used for all three holidays, not just one.

Your food shopping list will undoubtedly be the most complicated depending on what recipes you decide to cook, but in most cases, it will be rather similar each year. The autumn is a wonderful time to make the most of the new harvest, so pumpkins, turkeys, corn and so on are all going to be top of the list each year. We like to keep a 'master list' of foods we will need for all our holidays, then add to it as we finalize our menu.

A notepad and pen are always handy for jotting things down, but a digital list can be even better. Check out the website of your local supermarket to see if it allows you to create a customized list online, especially one that includes coupons you can clip before you go into the store.

You probably have a jotter in the kitchen to note down when you run out of any important ingredients, so you can replace them before you have nothing left. Check your jotter each week and either buy the item, or add it to your list. Add to your master list once you have finalized your menu.

Having a digital guide such as this one, that you can read on any device you own, is also a great way to stay organized. If you are worried that you do not have the right ingredients for a recipe, just look up the recipe your mobile device when you are inside the store.

Taking time to organize and plan ahead can lead to a lot less stress this Thanksgiving, and more fun for everyone. Hopefully your family, friends and relatives will all wish to contribute to a happy holiday, not a stressful one. But just in case, we hope you find all these stress-free holiday tips useful.

Take a few minute now before diving into the next chapter to gather all your resources together, including any notes that you have from previous years if you have hosted Thanksgiving before. Beginning filling in your worksheets, guest lists and so on, starting with yourself and anyone you live with, and their special dietary needs.

Then when you feel ready, on to the next chapter, planning the Thanksgiving menu.

Chapter 3: Planning The Family Thanksgiving Meal

Depending on your role in your family, it might be your turn to be in charge of the entire Thanksgiving meal for the whole clan this year, and you are looking for inspiration and shortcuts with the help of this guide.

Or you might be a first-timer who will be hosting at your new place and do not consider yourself to be much of a host or hostess, or cook.

We know what you are thinking: Can you pull it off?

Our guides are designed with beginner cooks in mind, for healthy, easy recipes without a lot of expensive ingredients. So the answers is YES! With a little bit of planning ahead of time, you can throw a great family Thanksgiving get-together without stressing out totally or being busy for weeks on end to prepare for just one holiday.

The key is advanced planning for all aspects of the day itself, from décor to dinner. We made a good start in the first chapter setting up our folders and starting to organize our guest list, notes on any special dietary requirements, and list of food items and/or chores to delegate to each reliable guest.

Your guest list has to be your first step, because it is almost impossible to determine how much food to buy and cook without knowing how many mouths you will be feeding. Contact friends and family early and request they RSVP by a certain date. Follow up with them in the weeks and days before Thanksgiving to make sure you know who is and isn't coming. Find out if they are bringing a guest, and if they have any special dietary requirements. Plan for at least 2 extra guests, or more if you are entertaining a larger crowd. And after all, what is Thanksgiving without leftovers? Better to have too much food, than too little. All of you readers who enjoy Mara's cookbooks will know she likes nothing better than make ahead and freeze recipes to pack her freezer with. If you do not own a deep freeze yet, consider buying one before the holiday season gets into full swing. (See Mara's <u>More Make and Freeze Recipes</u> for handy guidelines and 30 delicious recipes.) Yes, it will cost a fair amount of money to start with, but the savings can be considerable in terms of time and money and being able to cook in bulk, make your own meals from scratch, and parcel up the leftovers into home made 'TV dinners' your whole family will love. Thanksgiving is an ideal time for a big cook off, for meals that will feed the family while they are home from work and school for the holiday, and for a range of recipes that make the most of the bounty of nature at this time of year. Food prices are relatively cheap on some seasonal items. Turkey is also a very versatile protein, lending itself well to a range of dishes and cuisines.

As you plan your menu, you will refer to the notes you made when you were compiling your guest list. You should also consider your own tastes. It might seem really festive to have an entire bird for Thanksgiving, but if your family does not tend to like dark meat, just get a breast instead. If you are going to be feeding a large number of people and you know they like dark meat but your family turns their nose up at it, consider getting one whole bird and one breast.

In this way everyone should have plenty of what they like most, and you should also have a good amount of leftovers for sandwiches for one meal, and make and freeze meals you can eat and enjoy up to 3 months after you have cooked the turkey.

Your guests will also be bringing a range of dishes to contribute to the meal. Your guest list will be an invaluable tool to plan the menu for the day, and the leftovers. You will also have to plan for meals for the entire family while they are home from work and school, plus meals for any guests who may be staying.

If you are a member of a community group having a Thanksgiving get-together you will also be planning a contribution to take with you. Print out a copy of your Menu Planning worksheet you downloaded from the Resources section. Grab a calendar, pencil and some sticky notes.

Menu Planning for Thanksgiving and the Long Weekend

Once you know how many guests you'll have, then the fun begins. You get to start thinking about and organizing the menu and exploring delicious recipes. Turkey will be the central part of the meal in most households. Some might opt for ham or roast beef instead, but most people look forward to a hot turkey dinner once a year.

You can pencil in an additional entrée for vegetarians, or make a wide range of vegetarian and/or vegan side dishes that anyone can eat.

+Appetizers

+Main Dishes

+Side Dishes

+Breads/Rolls

+Salads

+Soups

+Desserts

+ Drinks, before, during and after

Organize any family favorite recipes in your computer and paper file folders. Make copies from your books so you have everything in one place. Start to pencil in the dishes you plan to serve for the Thanksgiving meal. Use the recipe index for this guide that you have downloaded to make sure you have items for each category. The index is hyperlinked at the end of this guide for your convenience.

Once you have planned the meal for the big day, work your way forward in relation to the leftovers, such as one round of turkey sandwiches for lunch the next day and perhaps another hot meal with turkey the day after. Your leftovers won't keep any longer than that, so any food you will not use in the 2 days after Thanksgiving should be frozen.

We tend to freeze it all right away to preserve freshness. In these days of microwaves, it is not a big deal to reheat and eat in a matter of minutes, compared to having a crowded fridge with food in danger of spoiling.

We know that not everyone loves turkey, but part of the reason for this, we find, is that they think it is dry and lacking in flavor. A badly cooked bird will be just that. For our bird, we promise it will almost be too juicy and succulent,, once you get the hang of it, and with no need for those expensive 'self-basting turkeys' that are really just pumped full of salt water and fat.

For the sake of this guide, we are going to assume a traditional Thanksgiving meal complete with a whole turkey, or a turkey breast.

The Turkey

A whole turkey creates a lot of food for people and pets in one oven over a period of a few hours. Best of all, very little needs to be done to it to make it come out tasting great. While it is roasting in the oven, you can be enjoying the company of your guests, decorating, or spending quality time with your loved ones.

While it is true that it does need to be carved, it is not that difficult a task once you become familiar with the anatomy of a turkey. These days there are excellent videos online that show you exactly how to carve a whole bird, including the breast.

The legs, wings, and even the back have good meat on them if you are prepared to wrestle with the skin. Once the skin has been removed, carve as much of the meat off the bones as possible, and then plan to cook the skeleton.

The turkey skeleton

As soon as the meal is over, and all the meat has been carved off the bones, don't waste a moment or a morsel of food. Place the skeleton in a large pot and cover it with just enough water to ensure nothing is poking out of it.

Boil the skeleton to make stock and/or soup. Pencil any soup you make as one of your meals for the weekend. Or, freeze the stock in one to two cup quantities to use in recipes that call for chicken stock. If you have made soup, create soup bowls in small plastic containers that can be heated in the microwave as part of a soup and sandwich meal. You can also freeze it and add a leftover roll for a complete meal. Use any leftover vegetables or starch in the soup as needed. For example, if you have some leftover rice, and a dish of peas, carrots and corn, let the turkey carcass cook down. Remove the meat from the bones and place it in a pot. Add the rice and vegetables and stir to combine. Then add enough stock to cover the ingredients. You can add more if you want a thinner soup. Add salt, pepper, celery salt, and perhaps some thyme, for your own homemade soup you can heat and eat the next day, or divide into portions and freeze.

The   stuffing

Stuffing can be one of the highlights of the meal if you make it well. Chestnuts are traditional, as are corn and herbs. The Pilgrims did not have a lot of wheat, so they would have used corn and herbs. Stuffing and bread crumbs were a good way to use up any stale but not moldy bread, so nothing went to waste. This is also the origin of classic bread pudding.

If you plan to stuff the bird, it will take on the drippings coming from the inner cavity of the turkey. You can also make it on the stove and serve as is. A compromise is to make it in a pot, then bake it to get the crispy consistency the outer part would get as it bakes in the bird cavity.

You can use bread stuffing, or cornbread stuffing. If using bread stuffing, look for whole wheat, or a combination of whole wheat and white. Beware of the instant packaged mixes, which are extremely high in sodium. So too are most chicken broths or stocks, used instead of water to give the stuffing a richer flavor.

The one other trouble spot in stuffing is the butter; some packages call for as much as two whole sticks if you are cooking the stuffing outside of the bird, in order to try to capture the flavor that in-bird stuffing gets from all of the juices from the turkey.

Some people also put sausage meat or small cut up sausage pieces into their stuffing. Again, with all the food you are going to be eating, this is perhaps adding a lot of unnecessary calories and salt to what could be a lighter dish. One alternative could be to lay some strips of bacon over the top of the turkey about 40 minutes before it reaches the end of its cooking time. This will give people who crave it the salty and smoked taste without overdoing it.

A lighter stuffing solution would be some butter, some olive oil, low sodium chicken or vegetable stock cubes, and some chopped celery, which will give the stuffing flavor and texture.

If you are cooking for any vegetarians or vegans, use soy margarine and vegetable stock.

The vegetables

Turkey is wonderful for many people at the holidays, but some of us enjoy the "fixin's" even more. Maybe it is the colors or flavors. Or perhaps it is the combination of sweet and savory, and all the delightful spices and seasonings that go into them.

The recommended daily allowance of vegetables and fruits is 2 ½ cups per day of each. It can be difficult to get anyone in the family to eat that much. The one exception seems to be Thanksgiving, when the veggies are devoured by everyone, even the fussiest of eaters. Pumpkin and cranberries are fruits, so just think how much nutrition you are getting, IF you hold back on the more fattening aspects of the traditional Thanksgiving side dishes.

Evelyn always finds it amazing that at Thanksgiving, most people take the incredibly low calorie bounties of nature such as pumpkin, corn, sweet potatoes, cranberries and green beans, and drown them in butter, cream, salt, sugar, and even marshmallows. But these tend to be traditional recipes that most people come to expect each year.

In this guide have created lighter versions of these. When you are planning your menu, try to offer some lighter, lower calorie alternatives to balance out some of the "heavier" traditional dishes. Also aim for a range of colors, green, white, orange, and so on, rather than, for example, white potatoes and white cauliflower to go with the white turkey.

Desserts

No special meal is complete without dessert of some kind. Pumpkin is the traditional pie, but you will also see apple and pecan. You might even see pumpkin cheesecake, or some other form of cheesecake. Pumpkin and apples are low calorie fruits, until you start to douse them with sugar, cream or cream cheese. Pecans are a nut, and as such are high in fat content, though they are also high in fiber and omega fatty acids. However, the sugar syrup that the pecan pie is smothered in, plus butter, and butter in the crust, can make this dessert a diet buster in more ways than one.

Calorie, Carb and Fat Counting

Speaking of eating light, let's remind ourselves of one of the most crucial differences between a whole turkey and a turkey breast. Some people love dark meat, some hate it.

More importantly, dark meat is far more fattening. For every 1 ounce of turkey, we are talking 1 gram of fat for the breast meat, versus 3 grams of fat for the dark meat. If you end up eating 4, 6 or 8 ounces of turkey, that would be the difference between 4 and 12, 6 and 18, or 8 and 24 whopping ounces of fat.

So if anyone is diet-conscious at your house, think about doing a turkey breast, and going light on the butter in all your dishes. Olive oil can still give flavor, but with no cholesterol. A balance menu means there will be something to eat for everyone. Use a good nutritional database like

http://ndb.nal.usda.gov/ndb/ or http://nutritiondata.self.com/ and calculate the calories, fat, saturated fat, carbs, fiber and protein in the dishes you are making.

Even if the recipe has already calculated them for you, do it yourself, and encourage the children to help you. In this way you will learn about healthier foods, with the ideal being a food that is low in calories and fat, but high in protein. If you are counting carbs, or just want to cut down on them, compare dessert recipes and opt for something with the least sugar.

Keep an even hand when you are cooking as well. For example, if you want to make a yam casserole with marshmallows on top, you can sprinkle just enough to cover the food, not smother it an inch deep. If a baking recipe calls for butter, swap half of it for olive oil, or in baking, applesauce. Here are some healthy eating substitutions from the Mayo Clinic

http://www.mayoclinic.org/healthy-living/nutrition-and-healthy-eating/in-depth/healthy-recipes/art-20047195 and here is a nice visual chart for baking substitution ideas. http://www.picklee.com/2012/08/01/recipe-substitutions/

Speaking of turkey breast versus whole bird, let's look next at how to do your turkey calculations once you have finalized your guest list.

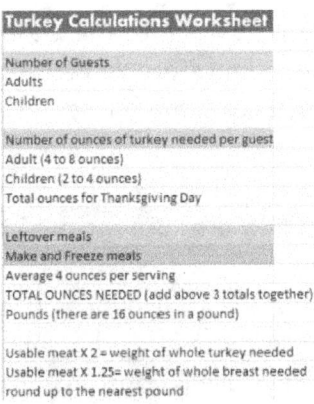

Turkey   Calculations

Once you know how many people you are expecting and approximately how many meals you would like to make from your Thanksgiving turkey, it is time to calculate how large a bird and/or breast you will need before you go to the store to buy them. Open your turkey calcaltions worksheet.

In reference to a whole turkey, for every 1 pound of turkey, calculate 50% wastage such as skin, bones, wings (not much meat on them) gizzards that they pack into the bird for gravy, and so on. You can still use these items for soup and gravy, but you will not be able to serve them as is to guests.

By this formula, a 12 pound bird would give you 6 pounds of attractive turkey meat. A 20 pound bird would give you 10. The larger the turkey, the more likely it is to be tough. You might be better off with two smaller turkeys, than one huge one, especially more than two members of your family like the drumsticks.

If you are not that fond of dark meat, but still have to feed a lot of people, opt for 1 whole bird and 1 or more breasts.

For a breast, calculate 25% waste for the bones and skin. A 10 pound breast would therefore give about 7.5 pounds of meat. They do not usually come packed with gizzards and so on so there is a lot less waste.

For each adult, calculate 4 to 8 ounces of turkey to be served.

For each child, calculate 2 to 4 ounces of turkey to be served.

Note down your turkey calculations on your worksheet and take it with you as you go shopping for your holiday bird.

Estimate 3 to 4 ounces of meat per person or meal you plan to serve with the leftovers. A healthy portion would be only 3 ounces, the size of a deck of cards, but that is unlikely at the holidays unless you decide to be really strict about it because you are watching your weight.

For example, if you are going to make turkey chili for 4 people, estimate anywhere from 12 to 16 ounces of turkey meat will be needed. Round out the dish with beans, tomatoes and corn, with tortillas, salsa and so on for a complete Mexican-style meal.

For a stir fry for 8 people, you would need 32 ounces of meat, or 2 pounds. Round out the dish with a bag or two of stir fry vegetables (you can get a good frozen assortment). Also add any leftover peas, carrots, corn and green beans (not casseroled) that remain from the meal and rice, or some noodles, and a dash of soy sauce and chili sauce for a Asian themed meal. Make and freeze any remaining food for your own TV style dinners.

One final reminder-a lot of turkeys are killed at this time of year, and if there are any fresh ones left over in the store, chances are they might go on sale the day after Thanksgiving. Consider buying another bird or breast for make and freeze meals. Once you see how easy it is to roast, you will never go back to expensive convenience meals again.

Once you have done your turkey calculations and filled out your worksheet, it will be time to go shopping. And in terms of planning your festivities for the day, it will be time to work out your turkey timetable.

Plan your Turkey Timetable.

Decide when you are going to serve the turkey hot to your guests, and work your way backwards using your turkey cooking chart and your turkey timetable, which you should have downloaded by now from the resources section and saved in your Thanksgiving folder with all of your other planning worksheets.

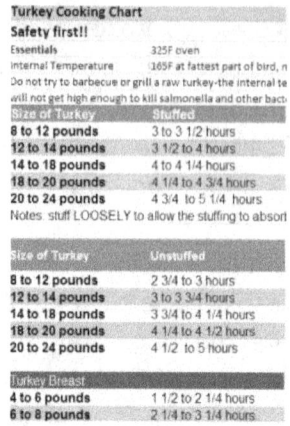

In your turkey calculations worksheet, you established how heavy a whole turkey and/or turkey breast you will need to feed all of your family and guests. Now look up the recommended time it will take to cook the bird safely so that no one will get salmonella or other form of food poisoning from the bird.

Once you have the total cooking time, carry it over onto your turkey timetable worksheet.

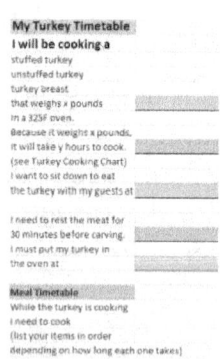

Allow 30 minutes for the meat to rest before carving. Allow at least 1 hour for appetizers, drinks, socializing and so on as people arrive, and as a cushion for any latecomers, up to 2 hours if you have a very relaxed family. The turkey can be resting as all of this is going on.

Most turkeys these days have a pop up timer that tells you it is ready, otherwise, use your meat thermometer. Take it out to rest as soon as it is ready, cover in foil and keep in a warm place while it rests. Put other items in the oven as needed, and finish off the rest of the dishes so that everything will be ready to serve at the same time.

One other note is that if you are baking a frozen pie, put it in the oven just before you all sit down to eat, if you have not already cooked it before.

Finalizing the Menu Plan

Know that you have your Turkey Timetable worked out, you have a notional schedule for the day itself, and some ideas for the other meals you will be eating that weekend.

Use your menu planning worksheet now to start filling in all the items you plan to serve your guests. Also pencil in leftover plans for the rest of the weekend as needed. Note down any other plans you might have, such as brunch at your church on Sunday, which means you will not have to cook an entire meal, but will need to bring something, which you might wish to cook in the morning, or perhaps the night before.

Look through your recipes and put them at the top of the folder, or in a separate computer folder, in order to make sure you have them all in one convenient place. Use the recipes in this guide for your inspiration, or to fill in any gaps. Photocopy or scan your recipes from your cookbooks and place them in your menu plan folder as needed.

Pencil in breakfast, lunch and dinner ideas for the others days you will be home, especially if you have guests staying with you. Use your own recipes, or sign up for our free ecourse on menu planning, which comes complete with instructions on how to plan menus effectively, plus handy recipes to suit all tastes.

Shopping Suggestions Before the Big Day

Consider investing in an <u>oven thermometer</u> and a <u>meat thermometer</u>. The oven thermometer will help you see if the number on the dial of your oven matches what the temperature is inside of it. Then you can adjust your thermostat accordingly to match the requirements of each recipe more accurately. We have cooked with ovens that have been as far out of kilter as 75 degrees too hot, or too cold, compared with what was stated on the dial.

A meat thermometer is a great food safety aid, since it allows you to determine the inner temperature of meat and poultry to make sure it has reached the recommended food safety temperatures. Poultry should be cooked to 165F to kill off salmonella. Measure it by inserting the end of the thermometer into the thickest part of the breast, not next to or on top of one of the bones of the bird, such as the leg. There is no such thing as rare poultry to eat.

If you do find it is very pink at the bone, either leave it as is for when you will be boiling up the bones for soup and stock, or slice it up and heat in the microwave until the flesh is no longer pink. Wash your knife with hot water and soap before starting to slice any other part of the turkey to avoid cross-contamination of bacteria from the undercooked meat to the cooked meat from the other side of the bird.

Thanksgiving Sample Shopping List

Turkey and/or turkey breast
stuffing such as Arnold or Pepperidge Farm (cubed)

Fresh or dried herbs
parsley
sage
rosemary
thyme

Fresh and Canned Produce

Fresh Vegetables
sweet potatoes
white potatoes
onions
garlic bulbs
1 large bunch of celery
corn on the cob
carrots
turnips
parsnips
beets

Shopping Lists

Once you have created a menu plan for Thanksgiving day, and for the long weekend, it is time to finalize your shopping lists. Having company over to your house can be stressful at the best of times, but catering to everyone's whims can be even more so.

But if you offer a variety of wholesome home-cooked dishes,

and plenty of salad and veggies, you should be able to please even the most difficult of guests this Thanksgiving. Nice desserts to round off the meal, such as cookies, cake and a pie, can also leave everyone happy and full, and impressed with your skills in the kitchen.

The autumn is full of the bounty of nature, so you can get some real bargains on food at this time of year. Use the suggested shopping list as the master list for your planned feast, and edit as needed by deleting and adding items depending on which recipes you are going to make.

Other Shopping Lists to Organize

Now that we have covered the essentials on what goes into a Thanksgiving menu, it is time to think about something other than food! It is time to think about cleaning and decorating the house in order to get ready for your great get-together.

On the second suggested shopping list, we have outlined items you will need for the party and for organizing leftovers, cleaning before, during, and after, and so on. We have also included a list of useful party supplies.

But one other reasonably urgent list will be in relation to any decorating needs you might have in order to get your home or party venue looking festive. Let's turn to the topic of decorating for Thanksgiving in the next chapter.

Chapter 4: Decorating For Thanksgiving

Decorating for Thanksgiving adds an element of warmth and fun to your home for the holiday. You don't have to go overboard, or put a lot of time or effort into decorating in order to make your house or apartment look festive. Getting the whole family involved can mean inexpensive but fun decorations you will cherish for years to come.

Your starting point is to take out any decorations you already have and make an inventory of them. Once you have made a list of what you have, decide where you are going to display them. Once you have displayed them, make a second list of items you would like to have, and whether you are going to buy them or make them. Use the worksheet in the Resource section to for the inventory and for your shopping list.

In terms of buying festive-looking items, they do not have to be expensive, and they can be practical. Some nice candles, napkins, table cloths and runners, can do wonders for a room and be suitable for use year after year if you do not light the candles.

Inexpensive serving platters, bowls and ornaments from your 99 cent store or local party supply store can also add just the right touch to your celebration. There are more durable items like soup tureens and bowls with fall themes, such as pumpkins, turkeys and so on. These might be a less expensive solution if they are not too costly and can be used year after year.

However, they might also break, and you would have to have enough room to store all your seasonal party ware in your home year after year. If you live in a small apartment, this will not be that practical.

One compromise is to dress up your plain plates each year with Thanksgivng-related food decorations or courses, such as little turkeys made out of salad items, or candy corn and so on. Serving family style platters of salads such as a green salad or fruit salad can also do double-duty as decorations.

Whether you are planning a sit down meal, buffet, or combination of both, turkey shapes can lend themselves to every part of the meal, from snacks to salads to desserts.

The only limit is your time and imagination.

A platter of pretty cookies can dress up any dessert table without breaking the bank compared to the cost of buying cookies from a bakery these days.

Nothing says autumn and Thanksgiving quite like a real pumpkin. You can use them for decorations as well as food too. Hollowed out mini pumpkins can even serve as a useful 'dish' for each guest, to eliminate some of the hassle of having to wash up after each course.

Put a label with each person's name on it and cover the writing with some tape to keep it waterproof. At the end of each course, all you will have to do is rinse them out before getting ready to use them again for the next course. Cut off the top to keep as a lid. Hollow out the rest to use the seeds and pumpkin flesh for a range of recipes. When cutting into the pumpkin to hollow it out, just be sure not to pierce the bottom or sides, so soup and so on will not leak when you serve it in the festive pumpkin bowl.

We will discuss table setting for the holidays in great detail below. For now, we just want to remind you of the range of options you have in and around the house, so jot down your ideas on your worksheets as you work your way through the next couple of chapters.

One of our favorite things about the holidays is the arts and crafts. Below you will find some suggestions as to how to quickly and easily turn your house festive for fall.

Yard   Displays

If you live in a house, there are endless possibilities for a yard display without spending a lot of money. The first is a wooden scarecrow, turkey, or Happy Thanksgiving sign.

For a little color, plant a few mums, either in the ground, or in pots and planters around the outside of the house. You can also place them along the pathway or drive leading up to your home.

To save money, you can invest in some realistic-looking fake flowers made of plastic, which should hold up well no matter what the weather and can be used again year after year if you wash them down at the end of each season, dry them, and then store them in a plastic bag to keep them dust-free.

Many people love to decorate with hay bales, colorful ears of Indian corn, or pumpkins in a range of colors. If you carve your pumpkin, it will spoil more quickly than leaving it whole. If you wish to paint your pumpkin instead with a range of scenes or saying suitable for Thanksgiving, you can then cover the pumpkin in plastic wrap to help weatherproof the paint. Use the painted pumpkin for decoration, then wash and eat it after Thanksgiving is over and you will start to get ready for Christmas.

But what if you don't have a great big yard? In that case, why not decorate your doorway??

Decorating Your Doorway

There are many different ways to decorate your doorway,, from a full porch full of items, to a simple wreath on the door to your apartment. Look at the space around the door and how much of it you would like to cover with decorations. A porch, especially a fully covered one with a roof over it, means you can create a great display just as you would in your font yard,but without having to worry so much about weatherproofing everything,

A door garland is an easy and festive way to decorate your door. You can buy ready-made ones created from a range of items, such as silk leaves or turkeys, or you can make your own with the help of the children and some construction paper, string, real leaves, and more.

Thanksgiving   Wreaths

Wreaths are lovely at this time of year. They are not just for Christmas any more. Mara has a wreath for almost every holiday, with seasonable items suited to the occasion.

Purchase or make a simple <u>wireframe wreath</u> and decorate it with fall leaves and miniature pumpkins. You can use silk leaves as well to make a wreath that will last for years. Add a nice bow in yellow and/or orange, and hang it on the front door.

You can also start with a basic ribbon wreath in a versatile color like gold. Wrap the ribbon around a <u>styrofoam wreath form</u> and then decorate the wreath each season or holiday with ornaments and other seasonal items such as flowers, leaves, bows and so on.

s

An autumn leaf wreath with real leaves will also work well, though the leaves need to be dry when you start gluing them onto your foam wreath shape. Acorns, nuts, chestnuts, and even pinecones can all beautify your wreath without you spending anything for the decorations.

Whenever you go for a walk around the neighborhood or the local beauty spot,. take a few plastic bags and some disposable rubber gloves. Pick up recycling and trash as you go along and put them into separate bags along with any other items you are able to collect, such as acorns from oak trees.

Once you identify some good trees to harvest, write them down in a safe place or in a file on your computer, so you can go back each year. Mara has a nearby pine tree that produces amazing amounts of cones every year. Evelyn has a favorite cluster of oak trees and one amazing horse chestnut tree that gives great big bristly chestnuts every year.

Leave the chestnuts as is, or shell the spiky out shell to get at the glossy reddish-brown nut inside to add even more variety to to your holiday decorations. (Note that these are NOT the same as the chestnuts you use for stuffing, so do not try to eat them!)

One other possibility is using mini gourds on your wreath. There are small real ones, of course, but you can also find an assortment of papier mache pumpkins and soon that will be much lighter in weight for hanging on a wreath. Their other advantage is that they will not decompose if left outdoors and exposed to extremes of temperature. Just make sure they are in a dry location.

Both real and craft gourds come in a range of colors and textures, from small mini pumpkins to bumpy and knobbled vegetables in all sorts of strange shapes. And don't forget the range of colors you can find in our trusty old fall friend, the pumpkin. They don't just come in orange, but tan, white, green, and even blue.

Of course, you will pay more for the most unusual varieties. A simpler solution might be to paint your entire pumpkin your color of choice using washable non-toxic <u>tempera paints</u>. Once it is dry, you can use it as the base for your decorating needs.

When you go into the craft or home decorating store to look for your mini gourds, you can also look for plastic or dried flowers. If you do want to use real gourds, you can find small ones in large bags in the supermarket each year. They will usually be placed near the pumpkin display. You should also find your ears of Indian corn there too.

While you are in the supermarket, look for bags of unshelled nuts such as walnuts and almonds, even peanuts. They can be stuck on wreaths and garlands to make them look more attractive. Once the holiday is over, you can shell them wash them, and then eat them. If you have any concern over germs, chop them up and cook them.

Whole peanuts can be strung on thread using a needle. So can cranberries and popcorn. The peanuts and cranberries can be washed, boiled and eaten after you no longer need the decoration. The popcorn can be fed to outdoor animals such as squirrels.

Regardless of whether you live in a house or apartment, a decorated door can really set the tone for any holiday gathering you will be hosting.

If you are willing to take a bit of time, and invest in a few inexpensive art supplies such as ribbon, styrofoam wreath forms, and glue, or a hot glue gun if you and your children love to do projects, you can create great holiday decorations for a fraction of the cost of store-bought wreaths and other decorations..

All of the natural items we have just mentioned, the pumpkins, leaves, nuts, and gourds, can also be used to create attractive displays indoors as well. Let's look in the next section at decorations for Thanksgiving that you will place inside your home.

Decorations Inside Your Home

Inside your home, the possibilities for decorating for Thanksgiving are almost limitless. Your only real restrictions will be space, budget and safety concerns. Some people like to decorate every room of the house. Others like to decorate the main rooms where the family spends the most time. Others might just wish to decorate the location where they will be hosting the holiday festivities.

Since of a lot of the Thanksgiving holiday is spent near or at the dining table, your dining room, if you have one, would be the best place to decorate. However, this can cause issues if the room is small and the crowd is going to be large. One compromise would be to decorate extensively the areas of your home that lead from the front door to the location you will be hosting your festivities. Treat the dinner table and/or buffet table as the extension of your decorations with pretty Thanksgiving-themed place settings.

One of the easiest ways to decorate for any holiday is to use a few items that are in the color of the holiday or season.

For example, you can change the entire look of your home with some fall-colored small pillows or throws draped on your sofa or your arm chairs. Fall colored candles and bowls of pot pourri with rich scents like pumpkin spice can transform a room easily, and be used year after year.

Mantelpiece   Displays

The mantel over your fireplace, if you have one, is the perfect place to decorate for Thanksgiving. For a simple display, arrange some pumpkins or decorative gourds and/or Indian corn on the mantelpiece, along with a few candles.

A fall wreath is a nice touch above the mantelpiece, as well as on your front door. A garland along the mantelpiece works well here too, as well as on your front door. Scarecrows, Pilgrim themes, and turkeys will also work well here.

Some people love ornaments and figurines. With many children in the house, plus pets, we tend to both steer clear of glass ornaments that might break if dropped, but you can mold ones out of clay that is then baked to set it hard, or cast using plaster moldings and then painted.

If choosing a plaster mold, check the pattern to make sure that some items are not too small and delicate, such as the beak or feet of the turkey, because the mold can get clogged or the item can get snapped off when you are unmolding it if you are not careful.

Other fun craft kits and skills to try include stained glass windows and glass painting. These can be hung over then mantelpiece or on a ribbon along it, or in the windows to let the light shine through them.

On any mantelpiece or table, a fall flower arrangement will work well as a decoration. Let's look at your options in the next section.

Fall Flower Arrangements

Cut flowers are lovely, but they are a waste in some senses because they will soon wither and die. Therefore, you might prefer a potted plant or even dried or silk or plastic flowers in a range of autumnal colors that will work well for the decorations you have in mind.

You can also use a plain vase and decorate it with fall items such as nuts. Or use a clear vase, fill it with gourds, nuts and so on, and then insert the stems of the flowers into the center. A bowl of colorful leaves will also word. Rest a small pot of flowers in them, or a candle in a holder. We use Pacific Soy Candles because they are so natural, smell great, and burn for a very long time. The Tuscan Blood Orange candle is a great orange color, perfect for the autumn.

Silk flowers or dried flowers may seem a bit pricey in the stores these days, but they will last for many years if you take care of them properly and do not allow them to get all dusty.

If you do end up with flowers at the holidays, such as gifts from your guests, enjoy them for a couple of days, then hang them upside down to dry them to use next year.

Pumpkins and Corn

You can make a beautiful fall arrangement by setting out some miniature pumpkins and ears of corn on your table or sideboard. Look for yellow, red, multicolored and purple varieties of corn for an authentic Thanksgiving feel. Scatter them across your dining table, or arrange them in a bowl for a nice centerpiece.

Cornucopia

Nothing says autumn and Thanksgiving like the Cornucopia, the Horn of Plenty. Get a large woven horn or make one yourself out of some cardboard or thick brown paper over a wire frame, and fill it with a range of colorful fruits and vegetables.

Display Your Kids' Artwork

The schools will be keeping children occupied with all sorts of fun seasonal activities.

Not only will your home be beautifully decorated, but you'll be building your children's self-esteem at the same time. Buy a few inexpensive frames and set them out or hang them on the wall. This is of course also a great way to display your child's artwork year round.

Everyone knows how to make a Thanksgiving turkey picture, by tracing their own hand with the fingers outstretched, then making it look like a turkey. Help your child with the details and coloring, and you will have some great art.

Theme: The First Thanksgiving

There are quite a few ways to incorporate the first Thanksgiving in your decorations.

Create a small scale version of this special occasion by setting out a few figurines of pilgrims and Native Americans. Complete the scene with a small table, some turkeys and miniature trees to show that the first Thanksgiving took place outside.

You can also find coloring books on the topic, or <u>free printables online</u>. Pphotocopy the pages, and then color them and cut them out. Mount them on little cardboard stands to make your own Thanksgiving diorama.

If they are small pictures, enlarge them, or if large, decrease them in size using a photocopier, and use them for a variety of purposes.

Pilgrim hats are associated with Thanksgiving, though there is little evidence that they were worn by our founding fathers. But they can still be a fun idea for dress up or table decorations.

Theme: Colonial Thanksgiving

The first Thanksgiving was a rather frugal affair compared to what we enjoy these days. One other historically based idea might be to research what people in Colonial times would have done to celebrate the occasion.

You can look up recipes online at the Williamsburg website. The American Heritage cookbook is out of print, but you can usually find a second-hand copy to explore a range of traditional dishes from the past two centuries.

You can find colonial paper dolls, cut them out and mount them. You can play dress up, with some frilly aprons and caps or tricorn hats you can wear as you all sit down together at the table. Look up George Washington's Thanksgiving Declaration and discuss what you all think his reasons were for making it.

With some cheap but attractive Thanksgiving decorations, you can quickly and easily turn your home into a lovely welcoming haven for the holidays. The only limit is really your imagination.

Once you have decorated the room, it is time to think a bit more about your table settings. Let's look at this topic in the next chapter.

Chapter 5: Setting The Table For Thanksgiving

When hosting Thanksgiving dinner for friends and family, the food is of utmost importance. However, if you serve the most decadent meal on flimsy paper plates that sag and collapse, your delicious meal will seem a bit less than spectacular.

It works both ways. If you invest some time and effort into decorating your Thanksgiving table -your overcooked turkey, and undercooked potatoes will be less noticeable. We eat with our eyes first, so a gorgeous table can really set the tone for your gathering, even if you are just sitting down with your own family. If you are throwing a party, your plain plates can be made attractive with visually interesting food presentations, particularly if you set out a buffet of appetizers and/or desserts. If you do not have a table large enough to seat everyone together, then you will create a buffet for the main course and side dishes as well.

While we certainly advocate making your life easier, and not running the risk of smashing the family china, there are ways to make your holiday table festive quickly and easily without spending ages washing lots of dishes.

The following are just a few suggestions.

Pumpkin Bowls

We have already outlined this idea above. Use small hollowed out pumpkins for your soup, appetizer and salad, for example. It will save on disposable items and just needs to be rinsed and returned to each person between courses.

Tablecloth

Bring out the good linens for your guests. If you don't have a Thanksgiving tablecloth, you can use some Thanksgiving or fall themed fabric. There are even some very nice looking fall and Thanksgiving themed disposable table cloths available. Just check your local party store, or a good linen store, or look online.

Or, if you want something more versatile and practical, get a tablecloth in brown, gold, or orange, and get a Table Cloth Runner with a Thanksgiving or autumn theme.

A runner with a harvesty theme will mean you can use the table cloths over and over again, and just vary the runners according to the occasion. Plastic or crepe paper table cloths will also work if you just want a quick clean-up.

You can also let the children make a paper runner decorated with their artwork, drawing, leaves and so on. They can make matching placemats as well if they wish.

Placemats

Placemats can range from pretty to practical, arty, to a fun way to keep the children busy while they are at the table. You can download the printable placemat above or encourage the children and each guest to make one of their own for the occasion at the craft table you will set up to help pass the time during the day.

Napkins

The napkins can be cloth or paper. They will also range in size from dinner napkins to small cocktail napkins.

Buy some orange, gold, or green cloth napkins. You can find these reasonably-priced at most discount stores. They will add a nice "holiday" touch to any table. Paper is also perfectly fine. Just make sure you have a variety of sizes, from dinner to cocktail napkins. They can all match, or you can use a rainbow of colors.

Thanksgiving   Themed   Centerpieces

A centerpiece can liven up any table, from the dinner table to a buffet table. It can be something as simple as a bowl of miniature pumpkins, gourds and Indian corn, or a fall flower arrangement.

If you have a cornucopia, or a wicker basket, fill it and lay it on the table, allowing some of the corn and pumpkins to roll out of it.

Other Festive Table Setting Touches

Little touches make a big difference. You could scoop out a pumpkin and serve dip in it. Use mini pumpkins with names written on them as place cards.

Use a hollowed out pumpkin as an ice bowl, soup tureen, or vase.

Turn an apple, some toothpicks and a few miniature marshmallows into a turkey. Start by setting the apple on a flat surface. Insert a toothpick with a large marshmallow on one side.

Add some raisins as eyes. For the turkey's tail, add four toothpicks with a miniature marshmallow on each end to the other side of the apple.

Voila - a turkey for each guest that also makes for a fun and healthy snack. Set the table the night before to free up time during the big day.

Serving Dishes

If you set a nice table, arrange for most of the food to be set out on a separate table, buffet-style. Consider getting hotplates, crock pots, and chafing dishes to keep food warm while it is sitting out.

Use attractive <u>themed serving dishes</u> for all of the food, for a more festive occasion.

Again, you can find the decorative bowls and platters, and chafing dish items, in a good party store. Just make sure you never allow children to go near chafing dishes, and beware of how hot the little heat cans can get.

The Dishes

The type of dishes you use is up to you. If you are mostly entertaining adults and this is a fairly small get together, it may be a good idea to use your fine china.

On the other hand, if you are entertaining a large crowd and have lots of kids in the mix, opt for <u>disposable dishes</u>, cups and cutlery. Clean up will be much easier and you don't have to worry about dishes breaking.

Paper plates are okay if they are the coated ones like Chinet, but you might want to consider plastic ones too. They are not as good for the environment, it is true, but many of them are recyclable once rinsed.

They come in a variety of colors, so you can go for orange and gold or brown, with matching napkins, and plastic cutlery, plus table cloths too.

I have found the plastic knives don't always hold up that well to cutting/pressure, so you might want to buy extra, or have sharper knives on hand for the adults. If you are having a sit down meal, obviously you will set the table, If you are having a buffet, make sure the plates, cutlery and napkins are all in a logical place at the start of the serving area.

Glasses and Cups

If you are serving wine, you will need the appropriate glasses, either real, or plastic. Have a variety of sizes of cups and glasses for juice, soda and so on if you are entertaining little ones as well. Make sure you have enough cups and mugs on hand for coffee and tea after the meal.

Other Advanced Preparations

Try to organize the coffeemaker to be switched on easily, and desserts baked and ready to serve before the guests comes. The desserts can be a decoration themselves depending on how fancy they are. You can get decorative cake tins which will shape your cakes-turkeys, a cornucopia, pumpkins and so on.

Multiple Courses, Multiple Plates and Cutlery

If you are having a sit down meal and doing appetizers and salad or maybe even soup first, and then will have to change plates for the main entee, make sure you have the right number of small plates and bowls, forks and spoons.

If you are using the smaller plates in your dish set for the salads, you can either have someone wash them to use them for dessert, or make life easier and just designate either plain glass dessert plates or paper plates so there is less frenetic activity in the kitchen and everyone can enjoy their meal.

Make sure you also have enough forks and napkins on hand for the dessert course.

Hopefully all these hints and tips will help make your Thanksgiving meal a happy and relatively stress free holiday.

Chapter 6: Planning The Perfect Thanksgiving Party

A Thanksgiving-themed party will in many cases be different from a formal sit down meal with your family. :It will be more informal in most cases, and might even be a buffet rather than a sit down meal.'

You can try to plan it carefully, or you might decide on a potluck or organized pot luck where everyone signs their name to a dish or category in order to be sure you have the essentials. You can provide the turkey/s, for example, while the guests bring the turkey, cranberry sauce and so on,

Or you might decide to forget the turkey and enjoy a range of fun finger foods and snacks as you play a range of games or enjoy activities with your guests.

Thanksgiving is usually considered to be a traditional family holiday, but remember that not everyone has family here in the USA. For visitors and newcomers to these shores, Thanksgiving can be a bit of a mystery, but everyone we have ever invited so they are not alone on the day has enjoy the traditional foods, football, floats at the parade, and so.

So don't be a party pooper and order pizza when there is so much pumpkin, pecan and other traditional delights to enjoy. They can actually work out cheaper due to the fact that it is harvest time and you can get great sales on many items.

And remember, you do not need to be superchef. With the Mrs. Smith's pies on sale for only $3 each instead of $7.59 at Evelyn's nearest supermarket in Manhattan, they are a bargain if they save you time and effort. Don't forget to stock up on the cherry, Dutch apple and blueberry at that price. After all, just think what 3 to 4 pints of blueberries or cherries would cost if you were to buy them fresh.

Once you decide on the day and the date of your party, you can go through the same process of organizing the guest list, making notes on food preferences, who is bringing what, and who will be reliable enough to delegate certain chores to.

If you are hosting a party as well as a more formal family gathering, that can mean double the cooking, or it can mean batch cooking and either holding the food over until the next day or so and then reheating it, or making it and freezing it.

This will be determined in part by what you are serving, and whether or not it will freeze well. It also makes a difference if you want some food to be hot, or if it is fine to eat it cold or at room temperature.

Remember, nothing can spoil a Thanksgiving party more than a burned-out hostess, so be sure to start planning your party well in advance and stay organized throughout the weeks and days leading up to your holiday celebration/s.

We use our master list of what needs to be done and when, and start cleaning and preparing ahead of time on the weekends or weeknights as we are able. In particular, we give trial runs to any recipes we have never tried before. There are several reasons for this.

The first is to see how the food is going to taste. We cook the recipe exactly as is and see how the chef intends it to come out. Then we make adjustments, if any are needed, to cater to the particular tastes in the family. The second reason is to see how long it takes to cook the recipe, and if there are any tricky parts to it.

A third reason is to make sure the recipe is written correctly, with nothing left out, or in the wrong order. A fourth reason is to make sure we have all the ingredients in the house. Shopping early and buying enough quantities for at least a couple of batches of the recipe means you do not need to dig in your pantry trying to find what you need, or desperately making substitutions that render a recipe that is supposed to be light and fluffy into shoe leather.

A fifth reason is to fill our freezers with a range of make and freeze recipes, because we will all be home a lot more, and we have said, we can test the recipes to see if they freeze well. If they do, we can then make as much of our meal ahead of time as possible and leave the items that do not freeze well or need to be served piping hot until the day itself.

A sixth reason is to have food on hand no matter who arrives. It is always easy to deal with extra food, but a good deal harder to cope with not having enough of everything if more people arrive than expected, or there are fewer items than you expected from the potluck (or they are not very good after all). Make and freeze meals with a festive flare, or traditional dishes one expects to have at Thanksgiving means everyone can have great food and not be disappointed with what is on offer.

One other reason in our houses is that we do a lot of charity work, and Evelyn always has foster children coming in and out all year round. Make ahead and freeze meals mean you can feed people well no matter who comes to the house. If the items are all parceled up, you can even send leftovers home with guests easily, especially if you know they don't cook, or are living in a place where cooking is difficult, such as a dorm or small bedsit, as we call them in England, which is a studio apartment in the US.

We also send home our own packaged up TV dinners with any guests we have invited to make sure they are not alone at the holiday. We let them choose what they want to take, with our families all secure in the knowledge that they will not be missing out on any of their favorites because they are in the freezer any time they need them.

Cooking ahead means you will always have good food available no matter what. Just be sure to label everything as needed to avoid confusion in case any emergencies arise.

Your timetable for a party will be the same as a formal dinner, with you organizing everything about 1 month in advance, or up to three months in advance if you plan your pumpkins to make sure you make the most of the harvest this year.

Keep your eyes out for bargains and frozen turkey or turkey breast, or any other items that you plan to serve for your party. Make room in your freezer ahead of time and load it up with bargains.

Don't forget extra tin foil, and more food storage containers, both for your own make and freeze meals, and for dealing with leftovers for people to take home.

The house should already be decorated as part of your usual list of preparations for the holidays.

Your menu plan should be based on the number of guests, ages, and degree of informality or formality for your party.

Use a blank menu plan and pencil in recipe choices for

+Appetizers

+Main Dishes

+Side Dishes

+Breads/Rolls

+Salads

+Soups

+Desserts

+ Drinks, before, during and after as needed.

One final point is if the food will be sit down, buffet, or a combination of both, such as an appetizer and/or dessert buffet and a sit down main course.

Food will be a large part of the focus of the day or any Thanksgiving party, but you can't spend all your time eating and drinking. Let's look in the next chapter at activities to do on

Thanksgiving Day or at your party to help the time fly by and take the stress out of the holiday.

Chapter 7: Thanksgiving Activities

You will be spending a lot of time with friends and family at Thanksgiving. While a lot of it might be spent cooking and eating, the whole point of Thanksgiving should be to spend quality time with the people you care about most.

Therefore, no matter how many people you are expecting to come and visit, it is always a good idea to try to plan some activities to make the time fly by and not cause yourself more stress wondering if everyone is having a good time.

The children will be out of school and restless, and probably excited about the holiday. Older relatives might not have a lot of energy or tolerance for noisy children. Your guests might not all know each other well, and you certainly do not want anyone to feel left out. Organizing a range of activities should help you solve all these issues.

Board games are always fun for kids and adults, such as Monopoly or Trivial Pursuit, such as the Party Edition. Or buy a DVD-style game like Scene-It or Who Wants to Be a Millionaire and gather around the TV for some trivia.

Then there are card games, or a Thanksgiving treasure hunt, coloring, word games and puzzles, and more.

Just for the Kids

Set up a craft table for the kids. Set out coloring pages and art supplies and let them enjoy themselves. Just be sure to put out some plastic aprons so they do not ruin any nice holiday clothes.

You can find lots of free coloring pages online. Just print a few of them for each child, and lots of crayons. That should keep them busy while you prepare the rest of the food.

Here are some good Thanksgiving printables:

http://www.scholastic.com/teachers/article/thanksgiving-printables
http://www.dltk-holidays.com/thanksgiving/printables.htm
http://www.abcteach.com/directory/holidays-months-and-seasons-holidays-thanksgiving-3654-2-1

You can use the pictures to make a treasure hunt inside the house or out in the yard. Give your guests clues to find puzzle pieces or Bingo pieces and fill their board, with prizes for the winners and all the teams that participate. Pair them up in teams, and switch the teams for each game.

Pin the Tail on the Turkey

Create a large turkey and feathers out of construction paper.

You can do this as one whole tail, or give differently colored feathers. The person who gets all 4 colors on the turkey the fastest wins. Use a stop watch on your phone and a pad to keep track. Make sure there are little prizes for the runners up.

Arts and Crafts

As your turkey cooks, you can all make arts and crafts projects together. Lay out pieces of orange, brown, and yellow construction paper and show the kids how to make a turkey by tracing their hand. Or have the kids make pilgrim hats out of black and white construction paper. We also like making them out of small plastic <u>plant pots</u>. Just cover the top with black paper and put a band and paper buckle around the edge. Or paint them and then add the colored accents. Add a brim and you have a great decoration you can use for your table.

Paper   Lanterns

You can adds some color to a room with a few simple paper lanterns made out of construction paper.

Make these out of strips of paper with holes punched into them that are held together with <u>brass fasteners</u>.

Enjoying   the   Outdoors

If the weather is not too cold or rainy, take the party outside for at least part of the day. A good walk before or after the big meal can stop tempers getting frayed, and work off some of the calories consumed on the day.

One of the staples of Thanksgiving is football. Traditionally, the men gather in the living room to watch the game while the women do all the cooking and cleaning. One way to keep the party lively is to give them a football and send them outside to toss it around during commercial breaks.

This can really get the men talking and having a great time. And, ladies - don't be shy. Jump right in there with them with tag football. Just make sure someone is keeping an eye on that cooking turkey... And be sure to delegate the washing up after the meal. If you've cooked, the least the guys can do is clean.

Party   Games

Charades, hide and seek, pass the parcel, hot potato, Simon Says, and so on, can all be played in company, with adults and kids alike. The important thing is to be together, and be thankful. Organize the games in advance and keep the party moving by having one person in charge of each game. Even the little ones can lead a game of Simon says and be proud that they get to act as a leader.

Thankfulness Activities

Thanksgiving is not just about food and football. It is also a nice time to take stock of all the things that you and your family have to be thankful for. Here are a few ideas to help your whole family count your blessings, not just on one day, but throughout the year.

Teaching Your Children to be Thankful

Thanksgiving is the perfect time to teach your kids about being thankful. Here are some ideas to teach your children how to appreciate the blessings in their lives, not just on Thanksgiving, but all year round.

Saying Grace

A good chance to list all the important people in our lives, and give thanks and special blessings to them.

Giving Thanks Placemats

The goal of this craft is to create a collage filled with drawings and pictures of all the things your children are thankful for. Cut photos from magazines, or print some photos from your computer.

Older children can write captions under the photos or draw their own. Be sure to put the child's name and the year on it.

If you make this collage from two standard letter size pieces of construction paper taped side-by-side, you can take the completed collage to a copy shop when you're done and have it laminated. It then becomes a placemat that you can use every Thanksgiving for years to come.

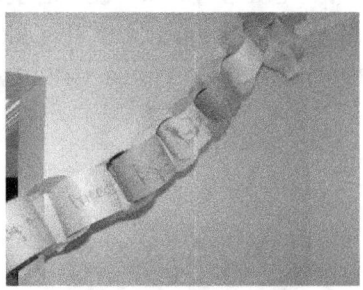

Thankful Paper Chain

Another way to remind your children of their blessings is to create a paper chain. This is similar to a regular paper chain - where you cut strips of paper and connect them together as loops, but there's one difference. You write on the strips of paper before you connect them.

Write the things you are thankful for with your children. For instance, "Grandma plays games with me" or "My teacher is nice," or just single words like friends, love, and so on

The fun part of this activity is to make the chain as long as possible - showing all your blessings. If you'd like to keep the garland on display until the end of the year up during Christmas, use green, white and gold paper as well as a few autumnal colors.

Thanksgiving Tree

This is another take on the idea above and works really well if you have several children in the family. Get each child to trace their hand on yellow, red, or brown construction paper. Cut out the hand shapes and write (or have the child write) what they are thankful for on the hand shape.

Cut a tree trunk shape out of brown construction paper. Glue it on a large piece of poster board. Let the kids add their hand shapes as leaves above the tree trunk, turning it into a beautiful fall colored tree.

Thankfulness Book

This idea is similar to the others, except it's more of a keepsake. Purchase a photo album or scrapbook kit and make a "blessings" theme.

Add photos of loved ones, including stories about why they are special to you.

Also, include pages about your favorite foods, favorite stories, favorite movies and all the other things that make you happy and thankful.

Any time you or your kids feel down, you can open your blessing book to see all the reasons you have to be happy, and thankful for the blessings in your life.

Tracing the Family Tree

If you have not already traced your family tree, now might be a good time to start this project. Unless we are full-blooded Native American, all of us are the descendants of people from other countries. Trace your ancestors to find out when they first came to the United States, what the country they came from would have been like, and so on.

With so many pretty autumn leaves, you can write the names of each person on a paper leaf and then pin it on the tree.

Volunteer at a Shelter, Food Bank or Soup Kitchen

At this time of year, many charities offer a hot Thanksgiving meal, shelter for a few hours, and fellowship to those who use their services because they are in need.

If you have any spare time, you and your older children (ages 10 and up, for example) can volunteer to help prepare the meal and/or serve it. A lot of charities are stretched to the limit in terms of volunteers and money. Their usual helping hands might have family commitments that take them away at the holidays, while others might come down with the flu and not be able to help as usual.

Working as a volunteer gives you a great feeling of doing something meaningful with your spare time. This kind of experience also helps you and your children feel more thankful for all of the advantages you have compared with those you help when you volunteer.

You can donate and/or volunteer online, organize a volunteer food drive and more at FeedingAmerica.org. You can also work with organizations like CityHarvest.org. They are hosting another 24 hour repackathon to parcel up bulk food donations into family sized packages for Thanksgiving and trying to set another world record of the number of pounds of food packaged in 1 day. Look for similar events in your area and get that warm fuzzy feeling that comes from helping others.

We hope the activities in this chapter will inspire you to organize a range of easy but fun activities that will take the stress out of the holiday and help everyone enjoy it more, with a mind of gratitude rather than taking everything for granted.

In the next chapter, you will find simple recipes to feed your family and guests without spending too much in terms of time, money and effort.

Chapter 8: A Traditional Thanksgiving Menu

In this chapter, you will find a range of traditional recipes to cover all aspects of the Thanksgiving meal without having to panic and stress that you are juggling too many things at once. Mix and match the recipes to make anything from a small family celebration to a large clan gathering or Thanksgiving party.

We will start with the stuffing, turkey and gravy as the main course for the meal. We will also be offering a number of dishes or variations of the recipes that will be suitable for any vegetarians or vegans.

1-Traditional Roast Turkey With Chestnut Stuffing And Homemade Gravy

Follow these instructions for a great meal the whole family will love.

Several Days or Weeks Before

Buy a frozen or fresh whole turkey, and/or a turkey breast that will be large enough for the number of guests expected, plus leftovers, using your Turkey Calculations worksheet.

If frozen, follow the instructions for thawing it in the refrigerator safely. Do not thaw outside of the fridge due to bacteria forming as the bird defrosts unevenly at room temperature.

The Night Before

If possible, the previous night, or at least one hour before you plan to cook it, prepare your turkey. Remove any giblets and rinse the turkey well inside and out with cold water. Pat dry with paper towels inside and out. Reserve the giblets for the gravy to accompany the meal.

Generously rub turkey with olive oil to keep it moist.

The Next Day

Preparing the Chestnut Stuffing

If you are going to stuff your bird, you will need to do this first. If you are going to serve the stuffing on the side so vegetarians and vegans can enjoy it, use vegetable broth and soy margarine in the recipe below, and do not add the egg.

1 1/2 cups whole chestnuts, or dried if you can't find whole
2 tablespoons olive oil
1 onion, peeled and minced
2 celery ribs, chopped
2 cloves garlic, peeled and crushed
1 teaspoon dried sage

1 teaspoon dried rosemary
1 teaspoon dried thyme
1 cooking apple, peeled, cored and thinly sliced
1/2 cup butter, or soy margarine, melted
1 egg, lightly beaten (leave out the egg if making a vegan version, or serving it as a side dish rather than in the bird)
1 1/4 cups chicken broth or vegetable broth
5 cups day-old stale bread (NOT moldy), cubed
Salt (sea salt is preferable) to taste
Pepper to taste

1. Preheat the oven to 375F.
2. Cut an X on the flat side of each chestnut.
3. Spread out on a baking sheet and bake 15 to 20 minutes.
4. Let cool for 10 minutes.
5. Peel and chop coarsely. Set aside. Note: Do not turn oven off as it will need to be preheated for cooking the turkey.
6. In a large pot over low heat, heat the 2 tablespoons of olive oil.
7. Add the celery and cook it for 3 minutes, stirring occasionally.
8. Add the onion and cook for 5 minutes or until soft and translucent, stirring occasionally.

Stir in the crushed garlic and cook for 1 minute.

9. Add the, sage, rosemary, thyme and apple. Cook for a further 3 to 5 minutes, stirring occasionally.
10. Remove the mixture from the heat.
11. Stir in the butter.
12. Add the broth and stir well to combine.
13. Add the egg if you are stuffing the bird. Omit if you will serve the stuffing on the side.
14. Add the chestnuts and bread cubes.
15. Stir the mixture up from the bottom to combine.
16. Season with salt and pepper.

17. Set aside until it is cool enough to handle as you stuff the turkey.
18. Or, if you are not stuffing the bird and are serving it on the side, cover it until ready to serve. Or, place in an oven-proof casserole and bake for 10 to 15 minutes or until crispy.
19. If you are stuffing the bird, stuff it LOOSELY. The stuffing will expand from the juices of the inside of the turkey as it bakes.
20. Once the turkey is cooked, remove the stuffing from the bird cavity, place in an oven proof dish, and either serve as is, or bake for 10 to 15 minutes or until crispy.

2-Roast Turkey

1 turkey (check your turkey calculations to be sure you have the right size of bird)
2 large carrots, cut into four
1 large onion, cut into four
3 stalks of celery, halved

1. Preheat the oven to 375F.
2. Remove your washed turkey from fridge.
3. Using the chestnut stuffing above, loosely stuff the neck cavity. If you are not going to stuff the bird, skip to Step 6.

4. Fold the skin under and secure in place with a toothpick.
5. Loosely stuff the main cavity, making sure to leave room for expansion and the air to flow through so the bird will cook fully to a high internal temperature so there is little risk of salmonella or other foodborne illnesses.
6. Prepare your roasting pan by spreading the vegetables over the bottom of it. .
7. Place a wire rack in the pan.
8. Place the turkey, breast side up, on the rack.

Add enough water to the pan to fill the bottom just up to the level of the rack.

9. Place the pan in the oven.
10. Bake the turkey, uncovered, for 30 minutes.
11. Remove from the oven.
12. Lower the oven temperature to 325F.
13. Using a <u>bulb baster</u> or a large ladle, baste your bird with the liquid at the bottom of the pan.
14. Lightly cover the breast with foil. Lightly cover the end of the drumsticks with foil so the thin 'ankles' do not get dried out or burned.
15. Place the turkey back in the oven.
16. Continue basting the uncovered parts of the turkey every 15 to 30 minutes depending on how long it has to cook. (Use your turkey chart to calculate the time it will take depending on the weight of the bird.) If the water level starts to get very dry, add another half cup or cup of water.
17. Thirty minutes before the time the turkey is supposed to be fully cooked, remove the foil and baste the entire turkey well.
18. Continue roasting for another 30 minutes, basting once at the 15 minute point.
19. Remove from the oven and cover with a fresh piece of foil.

20. Transfer to a platter for carving. Use a <u>turkey lifter</u> if you have one to avoid getting burned. Place the platter in a warm area to rest the meat before carving.
21. Reserve the liquid and vegetables from the bottom of the pan to use for the gravy (recipe below).

Turkey Cooking Charts

Size of Turkey   Stuffed
8 to 12 pounds   3 to 3 1/2 hours
12 to 14 pounds 3 1/2 to 4 hours
14 to 18 pounds 4 to 4 1/4 hours
18 to 20 pounds 4 1/4 to 4 3/4 hours
20 to 24 pounds 4 3/4 to 5 1/4 hours

Size of Turkey   Unstuffed
8 to 12 pounds   2 3/4 to 3 hours
12 to 14 pounds 3 to 3 3/4 hours
14 to 18 pounds 3 3/4 to 4 1/4 hours
18 to 20 pounds 4 1/4 to 4 1/2 hours
20 to 24 pounds 4 1/2 to 5 hours

Safety First-Determining if Your Turkey is Properly Cooked

To check if the turkey is cooked, use a meat thermometer on the thickest part of the thigh. The temperature should show at least 165F. Insert it in a thick part of the breast as well. The turkey should be golden and crispy on the outside too.

Remove the turkey from the roasting tray to a warmed carving platter. Scrape out all of the stuffing with a large spoon and place in an oven-proof casserole dish.

Cover the turkey with a new piece of foil, not the ones using for roasting, which have come into contact with the raw bird. Reserve everything in the pan for gravy (see recipe below).

Carving the Turkey

Rest the meat for 30 minutes on the carving platter. That is, do not carve and eat it right away, but allow it to settle down after being cooked, to release the full flavors and tenderness of the turkey.

When it is time to carve, start with the thigh bone to check for doneness. The juices should run clear without any pink as you cut it away from the body.

When cutting the breast, either create large slices by running your knife parallel with the breast bone of the turkey, or cut the entire breast away from the breast bone. Note that the flesh will flare outwards, so you will not be able to cut straight up and down. Angle your knife downwards and way from the bone, almost in a scooping motion, and pull away the breast meat from the bone with your other hand. If it gets stuck, use the pointed edge of the knife to cut through any clinging pieces of meat.

Dealing with the Wings

Either cut them off and put them on the serving platter, or leave as is for when you boil up the skeleton, for some extra meat that will be less tricky to get off the boil because it will be boiled until it falls off.

Once you have the breast off the bone, slice into small medallions, starting with the pointed side and cutting perpendicular to it, that is, width-wise, not length-wise.

Tip: For extra added safety, we like to remove the stuffing from the turkey once the turkey is cooked, and bake in a separate casserole dish for approximately 10 extra minutes, just to make sure there are no foodborne illnesses like salmonella lurking. You can't be too careful with poultry these days.

3-Roast Turkey Breast

1		turkey		breast
2	large	carrots,	cut into	four
1	large	onion,	cut into	four
3	stalks	of	celery,	halved

1. If frozen, thaw the breast in the refrigerator overnight.
2. Wash the turkey breast and pat dry.
3. Preheat the oven to 375F.
4. Prepare your roasting pan by adding the vegetables, spreading them over the bottom of the pan.
5. Place a wire rack in the pan.
6. Place the turkey breast on the rack.
7. Add enough water to the pan to fill the bottom just up to the level of the rack.
8. Place the pan in the oven.

Bake the turkey breast, uncovered, for 30 minutes.

9. Remove from the oven.
10. Lower the oven temperature to 325F.
11. Using a <u>bulb baster</u> or a large ladle, baste the breast with the liquid at the bottom of the pan.
12. Lightly cover the breast with foil.
13. Place the turkey breast back in the oven and continue cooking according to the time on the turkey cooking chart (in your set of downloads, and listed below), minus 30 minutes. Look in the oven every so often to check that the water level does not get too low. If it starts to look dry, add another half cup or cup of water.
14. Thirty minutes before the time the turkey breast is supposed to be fully cooked, remove the foil and baste the entire breast well.
15. Continue roasting for another 30 minutes, basting once at the 15 minute point.
16. Remove from the oven.
17. Cover with a fresh piece of foil.
18. Remove the breast from the pan to a platter. Use a <u>turkey lifter</u> if you have one to avoid getting burned. Place the platter in a warm area to rest the breast before carving.
19. Save the liquid and vegetables from the bottom of the pan to make the gravy (recipe below).

Turkey Breast Cooking Chart

Breast Size, Time to Cook

4 to 6 pounds 1 1/2 to 2 1/4 hours
6 to 8 pounds 2 1/4 to 3 1/4 hours

4-Turkey Gravy

giblets
water
pan drippings from cooked turkey or turkey breast
vegetables from the roasting pan after the turkey or breast is cooked
1 to 2 cups chicken or vegetable stock (optional)
1 to 2 tablespoons butter (optional)
splash of red wine (optional)

1. Using the giblets from the whole bird as your base if you have purchased a whole turkey, place the giblets in a large saucepan.
2. Add water to the giblets, just enough so they are fully covered.
3. Bring to a boil over a medium flame.
4. Lower the heat and simmer for at least 30 minutes, until the giblets look cooked and the liquid has reduced to about 1/4 less.
5. Remove the giblets from the pot. Set aside in on a plate to cut up for pet food, or discard once they are cool so they do not melt your trash bag.
6. Once your turkey or turkey breast is cooked according to the recipe above, either mash the vegetables remaining in the bottom of the roasting tray, or run them through a food processor or blender until completely smooth.

7. Place the vegetables and any remaining liquid from the pan into a saucepan. If you don't have a lot of liquid remaining, add 1 cup or more, depending on how much gravy you need, of low-sodium chicken stock or vegetable stock. Stir well to combine.
8. Bring the mixture to a rolling boil.

For a richer gravy, add 1 or 2 tablespoons of butter or margarine.

9. Reduce the heat and simmer over a medium flame for 5 minutes until fully heated through.
10. If desired, add a splash of red wine and cook and additional 5 minutes. It will give a richer taste but the alcohol will cook off so even the children can have some.

This gravy should have good body from the vegetables, but if you would like it even thicker, follow these additional steps.

Thickened Gravy

1-While the mixture is simmering, in a small bowl, add two tablespoons of cornstarch and whisk with 1/2 cup cold water until all lumps dissolve.

2-At the end of 5 minutes, slowly add the mixture a little at a time to the saucepan, stirring constantly.

3-Continue to add the cornstarch mixture until it is fully incorporated. Continue cooking the gravy, stirring constantly, until it reaches your desired thickness.

Hint:

Hate the grease in turkey gravy? Detest lumps? Then use a gravy boat with a bottom spout, as pictured above, or a grease separator, as pictured below.

Strain the gravy through the top. Once it is in the cup, the grease will float to the top and the gravy will sink to the bottom. Just squeeze the handle gently to pour the gravy. Set it on the table with a plate under it to stop drips and spills.

Make and Freeze

This recipe should freeze reasonably well, though the thicker gravy might separate a little bit when it defrosts or is reheated. Allow it to cool fully, and add on top of any turkey you are placing in make and freeze containers for your own TV dinners.

Or, freeze in a plastic container, allow to thaw overnight, and heat on top of the stove, stirring often, until any wateriness disappears.

Dealing with the Giblets

The giblets are the offal of the bird, and can include neck, heart, liver and kidneys. There is enough meat on these to make them a worthwhile treat for your dogs. Once they are cool, cut them up into small pieces. Carve any flesh you can manage.

Because the meat is so rich, only use a couple of spoonfuls at a time to supplement their regular food. In terms of turkey, limit the amount of dark meat they eat, for the same reason. They can enjoy turkey breast without any stomach or health issues.

Reminder: NEVER give poultry bones to dogs or cats. The bones can splinter and cut their mouth and/or gums and even puncture something in their digestive tract as it travels along. Even a small bone chip can kill.

Wrap the neck and the carcass well in old newspaper, wrapped tightly in a taped plastic bag (using duct tape or masking or packing tape) to stop animals inside and outside your home from rummaging in the trash and putting themselves in danger. If you have wildlife that tends to knock over your bins or get the lids open, consider weighing the cans down with some bricks.

5-Homemade Cornbread

Cornbread can be served on the side instead of or in addition to rolls. This recipe can also be used as the basis for cornbread stuffing.

If you would like to make a cornbread crust pizza to use up some of your leftover turkey during the long weekend, you can also use this recipe. Divide it over two 9 x 13" pans instead of just one, for 2 pizza crusts.

canola	oil	for greasing	the	pan
3	cups	yellow		cornmeal
1	cup	all-purpose		flour
2	tablespoons			sugar
2	teaspoons	baking		powder
1	teaspoon	baking		soda
1 1/2	teaspoons			salt
1/2 cup	butter	or margarine,		melted
3	large	eggs,		beaten
2 1/4	cups	skim		milk
1 cup	0% fat	plain		yogurt

1. Preheat the oven to 425F.
2. Grease a 9 x 13" pan with canola oil. Set aside.
3. In a large glass bowl, sift the cornmeal and flour, the sugar, baking powder, baking soda, and salt.
4. In a medium glass bowl or measuring cup, whisk together the butter or margarine, eggs, skim milk and yogurt until well combined.
5. Using the whisk, beat the liquid mixture into the dry ingredients a little at a time until completely combined.
6. Pour the batter into the pan and smooth the top.
7. Bake for 30 minutes, or until fully set in the center and golden brown on top.
8. Remove from the oven and place on a wire rack to cool for at least 30 minutes.

Cut into small squares to serve as rolls.

9. Or, use the cornbread for the cornbread stuffing recipe that follows.

Variations

If you use as a pizza crust, use 2 pans and halve the time you bake the crust. Top with your choice of sauce, toppings and cheese.

Make and Freeze

This recipe will freeze well. Allow to cool fully, cut up the cornbread, and freeze in the pan. Remove the cornbread and place in individual baggies. Place the small baggies into a larger zippered one. Remove a piece from the freezer any time you need a quick bread. Defrost in the microwave for 30 seconds, or allow to thaw at room temperature for 30 minutes.

6-Cornbread Stuffing

Cornbread stuffing is closer to what the Pilgrims would have enjoyed with the Native Americans who were helping them at the first Thanksgiving. It is a tasty alternative to chestnut stuffing and can be served outside the bird, making it ideal for vegetarians. The recipe has eggs in it, so is not suitable for vegans or anyone allergic to eggs.

Canola oil for greasing

1 loaf of cornbread (see recipe above)

3 cups day-old bread, cubed
1/4 cup butter
1 large onion, diced
6 large stalks celery, green only, diced finely

1/2 cup finely chopped fresh sage or thyme, or a combination of both
2 teaspoons black pepper
dash salt
dash celery salt
2 eggs, lightly beaten
6 to 7 cups low sodium chicken broth or vegetable broth, warm

1. Preheat the oven to 375F.
2. Grease a large casserole dish or baking pan with canola oil. Set aside.
3. In a large glass bowl, using clean hands, crumble your loaf of cornbread.
4. Add the bread cubes and toss with your hands to combine.
5. In a large frying pan, melt the butter.
6. Add the celery and cook for 3 minutes, stirring occasionally.
7. Add the onion and cook for 5 minutes, stirring occasionally. until the onion start to turn soft and clear.
8. Add the sage and/or thyme, black pepper and the two salts. Stir well.

Give the eggs one last beat and add to the cornbread mixture in the bowl.

9. Add the vegetables to the cornbread mixture. Stir to combine.
10. Add the broth, Stir well to incorporate fully.
11. Scrape the mixture into the prepared pan.
12. Bake, uncovered, for 35 to 40 minutes, or until it looks golden-brown and crispy.
13. Remove from the oven, cover with foil, and let cook on a wire rack for 15 minutes.
14. Serve hot on the side of the turkey.

Make and Freeze

This recipe will freeze reasonably well, as long as the stuffing is not too soggy. Portion out into your own make ahead and freeze meals, or allow to cool and place in a plastic container. Reheat in the microwave and fluff with a fork.

7-Classic Shrimp Cocktail

Shrimp cocktail is a lot easier than most people think. It can also be affordable if you buy a large frozen block with a 21 to 25 count. You can usually buy them at Asian supermarkets. Once you have defrosted the block under running cold water in the sink, cook up all the shrimp, which can then be eaten at the time, or frozen and used in a range of recipes such as stir fry.

This recipe needs to be made about 2 hours in advance of your intended serving time to allow the shrimp to get cold after being cooked.

Serving   Sizes
Allow at least 4 shrimp per person. You can multiply this recipe as needed. Four shrimp has only about 90 calories, but lots of protein.

32 large shrimp, shelled (see note below if you are not sure how to do this) and well chilled

1 pot boiling water

Cocktail Sauce
1 pound fresh tomatoes, cored and cut into quarters
1/2 cup white wine vinegar
1 tablespoon lemon juice
1 dash chili powder
1 teaspoon sugar
dash fresh black pepper
dash salt
1 tablespoon olive oil
Dash Old Bay seasoning
4 tablespoons prepared horseradish, such as Gold's (you will find this in the refrigerator section of your supermarket)

Greens of your choice, such as iceberg lettuce

Lemon wedges for garnish, if desired

1. Be sure the boiling water has reached a full rolling boil.
2. Place the shrimp in the boiling water. Reduce the heat to medium and simmer for 4 to 5 minutes, or until the shrimp look completely pink.
3. Drain the shrimp into a colander. Shake well to drain and place the shrimp in a bowl. Place in the refrigerator to chill for at least 1 hour.
4. While the shrimp are in the refrigerator, make the cocktail sauce. In a blender or food processor, process the tomatoes until smooth.
5. Add the vinegar, lemon juice, chili powder, salt, pepper, olive oil, and Old Bay seasoning. Process until smooth. Scrape out into a small serving bowl that will fit in the center of the platter you plan to serve the shrimp on.

6. Using a spoon, stir in the horseradish until well combined.
7. Place the cocktail sauce in the refrigerator to chill.
8. On a large serving platter, arrange your greens to form a bed. Leave a space in the center for your bowl of cocktail sauce. Place in the fridge to chill.

When you are ready to serve the shrimp, place the cocktail sauce in the center of the platter.

9. Arrange the shrimp on top of the lettuce. You can make a patter with them, such as tail side out and all facing in the same direction in a spiral around the bowl of sauce, for example.
10. Garnish the platter with lemon wedges, if desired.
11. Serve immediately.

Note: To shell shrimp, either use kitchen scissors or a knife. Start at the widest part of the shrimp and cut along the outer curve. Remove the shrimp from the shell, being careful of the tougher part, the tail. You can leave it on if you wish, for people to use as a handle, so to speak, when they are eating, or gently take the shrimp in one hand and the tail in the other and pull them apart with a steady tug.

Make and Freeze

The shrimp will freeze well once it is cooked. The cocktail sauce will not. Use the frozen shrimp as is in stir fry, soups, and so on. Or thaw for about an hour in the refrigerator to eat as is.

8-Apple, Onion and Squash Tart

This will make an attractive appetizer, or a vegan main course. It will serve 4 as a main dish, or about 12 to 16 as an appetizer depending on how you cut it.

1 large baking sheet
1 large piece of foil to line your baking sheet

1 all-butter pie crust (see recipe below)
2 tablespoons whole-grain mustard or Dijon mustard
1 large tart apple, such as Granny Smith
1 small or 1/2 medium butternut squash (about 3/4 pounds), halved, seeded, and skin off
1 small yellow onion, peeled, root end trimmed but otherwise whole
3 tablespoons unsalted butter, melted
1 teaspoon dried rosemary
1 teaspoons dried thyme
dash salt
dash freshly ground black pepper

1 large piece of foil to cover the tart fully

2 ounces low fat white cheddar cheese (medium or sharp), shredded, (optional)

1. Preheat the oven to 400F.
2. Line a baking sheet with foil. Curl up the edges slightly so you will be able to grab them easily later without burning your fingers on the pan.
3. Place the pie crust in the center of the baking sheet and flatten it out with the palm of your hand to resemble a pizza. Curl up the edges slightly as with a pizza crust.
4. Spread the mustard all over the bottom of the pie crust. Set aside.
5. Core the apple with a corer. Cut in half.
6. Cut each apple half into 8 slices and place them into a large glass bowl.
7. Cut the onion into slices so that they are about the same size as the apple slices. Add to the bowl.
8. Cut the squash into 1 inch cubes. Add to the bowl.

Add the butter, rosemary, and thyme. Toss gently to combine.

9. Season with salt and pepper and toss again.
10. Transfer the vegetables from the bowl to the top of the prepared pie crust.
11. Spread them out evenly and arrange the apple and onion decoratively if you wish.
12. Bake in the oven for 10 minutes.
13. Lower the heat to 375F.
14. Cover the tart with the second piece of foil. Fold up the edges from the first piece at the bottom of the pan to form a sort of foil envelope.
15. Bake the covered tart for another 45 minutes or so, until testing with a fork shows the squash to be quite tender.
16. If using the cheese, sprinkle it on top now.

17. If not, bake uncovered for another 10 minutes until the tart is nicely browned.
18. Cool on a wire rack for about 15 minutes to let it settle, 25 minutes if you used the cheese, so no one will burn their mouths.
19. Cut into portions with a pizza cutter or sharp knife and serve.

Make and Freeze

This recipe will freeze well. Allow to cool and freeze flat on the baking sheet. Place in plastic freezer bags. Thaw at room temperature for about 30 minutes to have a handy snack or meal any time. Or reheat in the microwave for 1 to 2 minutes, let stand for 1 minute, eat and enjoy.

9-Stuffed Portobello Mushrooms

These are a handy finger food if you choose mushrooms with smaller caps, or can serve as a vegetarian or vegan entrée if you serve mushrooms with larger caps.

4 or 8 medium portobello mushrooms, any stem trimmed off; cut the ends of the stems off and set aside to use as part of the stuffing
2 tablespoons olive oil
1 large yellow onion, diced

2	medium	zucchini,	diced
1	red	pepper,	diced
6	sun dried	tomatoes,	chopped
2	cloves	garlic,	minced
1 cup	of fresh	spinach	leaves
1	teaspoon	dried	oregano
1/2	teaspoon	dried	basil
dash	crushed	red pepper	flakes
freshly	ground black	pepper, to	taste
1/4 cup	seasoned low sodium	breadcrumbs, such as	4C
1	cup of	cold	water
1/4	cup shaved	Parmesan	cheese
1/4	cup low fat	mozzarella	cheese

1. Preheat your oven to 375 degrees.
2. Line a baking sheet with parchment paper.
3. Rub each mushroom with a bit of olive oil and set them on the sheet, gill side up.
4. In a large skillet over a medium high flame, heat the olive oil.
5. Add the onions and sauté for 3 minutes, stirring occasionally, until they start to soften and turn clear.
6. Add the zucchini and cook, stirring occasionally, for 5 minutes.
7. If you have any stems from the mushrooms, slice them finely and add them. Stir well to combine.
8. Add the red pepper and cook for 3 minutes.

Add the tomatoes and cook for 2 minutes, stirring occasionally.

9. Add the garlic. Cook for 1 minute.
10. Add the spinach and cook until it just starts to wilt, about 3 minutes, stirring occasionally.
11. Remove the pan from the heat and add the oregano, basil, red pepper, black pepper, and breadcrumbs.
12. Stir well to combine fully.

13. Divide the mixture evenly across the number of mushrooms you are planning to stuff.
14. Place in the oven.
15. Add 1 cup of cold water to the pan.
16. Bake for 20 to 30 minutes depending on the size of the mushrooms. You do not want to let them get dried out.
17. Top each mushroom with some of the cheese and cook for an additional 10 to 15 minutes until the cheese has fully melted.
18. Remove the pan from the oven and cool on a wire rack for 10 minutes.
19. Serve as is or with additional shaved Parmesan and finely chopped spinach sprinkled on top as a garnish.

Make   Ahead

These can be made the day before and rewarmed in the oven, but because of the high water content of mushrooms, they will not freeze well.

10-Roasted Beet, Orange and Onion Salad

1 pound small beets, preferably very small ones
1 tablespoon extra-virgin olive oil
Dash salt
Dash freshly ground pepper
1 cup pearl onions, about 1/2 pound, or 1 yellow onion cut into wedges
a splash of extra-virgin olive oil
Dash salt
Dash pepper
2 large oranges, peeled and divided into segments, or 2 large cans of mandarin orange segments packed in juice for a sweeter taste
3 tablespoons olive oil
6 tablespoons white vinegar
1 teaspoon dried basil
1/2 cup orange juice, with or without pulp
1 to 2 ounces feta cheese, cubed, or 2 ounces soy cheese, crumbled

1. Preheat the oven to 400F.
2. Wash the beets well.
3. Cut the tops and tails off the beets. Do not peel.
4. Line the bottom of a baking pan with foil.
5. Place the beets in the pan. Toss them with half of the olive oil, salt and pepper.
6. Add 1 cup of water to the pan.
7. Roast the beets for 20 to 25 minutes, or until a fork pierces them easily.
8. Remove from the oven, place the beets in a bowl, and place the bowl in the refrigerator to allow them to cool enough to handle safely, about 15 minutes.

Set the roasting pan aside for a moment.

9. Place the pearl onions or onion slices in a small bowl and toss with olive oil, salt and pepper.

10. Place in the roasting pan and bake for 15 minutes.
11. Turn off the oven and leave the pan in while you peel the beets.
12. Peel the beets, then cut in half and then into thin wedges.
13. On your serving platter, arrange the orange segments and beet slices around the platter, alternating one with the other, overlapping slightly, until they go around in a full circle.
14. Remove the onions from the oven and cool on a wire rack for a few minutes while you continue with the recipe.
15. In a small bowl, whisk together the oil, vinegar and orange juice. Add the seasonings and taste. Adjust as needed.
16. Place the pearl onions around the circle of oranges and beets so they look decorative, or sprinkle the onion over the top. Drizzle some of the dressing on the salad and serve the rest on the side in a small bowl with a spoon.
17. Sprinkle the feta cheese or soy cheese on top and serve with some crusty bread or a homemade flaky biscuit (see recipe later in this guide).

Make and Freeze

Due to the dressing and high liquid content, this recipe will not freeze well. It can be made a day or two in advance and refrigerated, covered, until you are ready to serve it.

11-Butternut Squash Soup

This soup will take about 2 hours to make, so plan your cooking timetable accordingly. It is a typical autumn dish which also makes the most of all the cheap, fresh produce at harvest time.

aluminum foil
1 large baking sheet

2 medium-sized butternut squash, washed well
1 to 2 cups water
1 large Granny Smith apple
1 tablespoon butter or soy margarine
1 medium yellow onion
2 teaspoons dried sage, thyme, or both
1 teaspoon nutmeg
1 teaspoons sea salt
1/2 teaspoon freshly ground black pepper
3 cups low-sodium vegetable broth
2 cups water
1/3 cup Greek style yogurt, or soy yogurt
1/2 cup toasted croutons for garnish, or some shelled pumpkin or shelled sunflower seeds (optional)

1. Place one oven rack in the middle of the oven.
2. Preheat the oven to 425F.
3. Prepare one large baking sheet by lining it with foil. Set aside.
4. Cut the two squash in half lengthwise.
5. clean out the seeds with a sturdy spoon, being sure to get rid of all the membrane.
6. Wash the inside well also.
7. Place the cleaned squash halves onto the prepared baking sheet, cut side down.
8. Place the squash on the rack in the oven.

Add 1 to 2 cups of water to the pan, being careful not to let it overflow.

9. Bake the squash for 45 minutes to an hour, or until the neck of the squash is tender when you pierce it with a fork.
10. About 30 minutes into the roasting time for the squash, wash, peel, core, and cut the apple into medium-sized pieces.
11. Cut the onion into 4, then chop coarsely.
12. In a large soup pot or Dutch oven, melt the butter over a medium flame.
13. Add the apple and onion and cook for 5 minutes, stirring occasionally, until they are softened.
14. Add the sage, nutmeg, salt, and pepper. Stir well to combine.
15. Add the broth and water and reduce the heat to simmer over a low flame.
16. When the squash is fork-tender, remove the pan from the oven and place on a wire rack. Allow to cool until you can handle the squash safely, about 20 minutes.
17. Using a large spoon, scoop the flesh into the soup pot and stir well to combine. Note: Do not scoop in the stem or the hard bottom of the squash. Discard the skins.
18. Increase the flame to high and bring the soup to a rolling boil.

19. Stir well and lower the flame to medium. Simmer, stirring occasionally to break up any large chunks of squash, for about 15 minutes.
20. Remove the pan from the heat.
21. Using a blender or food processor, and another large soup pot, purée the soup in batches until completely smooth. Pour each batch into the second soup pot.
22. In the final batch, add the Greek style yogurt and process until completely combined.
23. Pour the yogurt batch into the soup pot.
24. Over a low flame, reheat the soup, stirring well to incorporate all of the batches.
25. Season with salt and pepper to taste.
26. Serve hot in small cups or bowls with your garnish of choice, if desired.

Make and Freeze

This recipe will freeze well. Place in plastic containers with a roll or some crumbled crackers, for a handy soup bowl you can take and eat anywhere.

Or, reheat in the microwave for 1 minute, stir, heat for 1 minute, let stand for a minute, and serve with crusty bread,

12-Classic Cream of Mushroom Soup

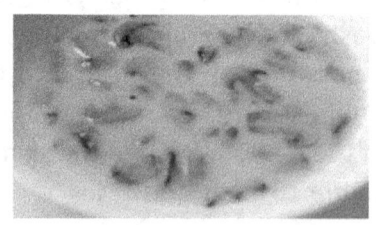

Many recipes for green bean casserole call for canned soup, which is high in sodium. In this recipe, you will be making your own from scratch. Use it as an appetizer for your guests, serve in small cups or bowls, or hollowed out mini pumpkins, or use as the sauce base for your Green Bean Casserole (recipe below). Leave the mushrooms chunky for your guests, or blend/process until completely smooth for the sauce base. This recipe will serve 2 to 4 as a soup, so multiply as needed.

1	tablespoon	butter
2	tablespoons	olive oil
1	tablespoon finely diced	onions
1/2 cup	button mushrooms, washed well and cut into slices	
3	tablespoons all-purpose	flour
1/2	cup skim	milk
1/2	cup vegetable	broth

1. In a saucepan over medium heat, melt the butter.
2. Add the olive oil.
3. Add onions and cook until soft, about 5 minutes.
4. Add the mushrooms and cook until they start to sweat, that is, release their juices, about 5 minutes.
5. Whisk in flour and cook for 1 to 2 minutes. Be sure not to scorch or burn it.
6. Slowly whisk in the skim milk and then the broth a little at a time, stirring constantly to avoid lumps.
7. Cook over medium to low heat, stirring often, until the soup reaches your desired thickness.
8. Either stir well and serve as is with some crusty bread or some croutons, or use as part of the sauce for your green bean casserole.

Notes: This recipe makes the equivalent of 1 can of store-bought condensed cream of mushroom soup. Multiply the ingredients by the number of cans any recipe calls for.

Variations:
You can substitute celery or chicken for the mushrooms to make your own homemade versions of those popular cream soups as well. Leeks or leek and potato would be two other good variations. If you are using chicken, substitute your homemade chicken broth for the vegetable stock.

Make and Freeze

This soup will freeze well for up to three months.

13-Classic Green Bean Casserole

1 portion of the classic cream of mushroom soup recipe (above)

4 cups frozen French style green beans
1 cup skim milk
Dash pepper
Dash celery salt
1 1/4 cups French fried onions (canned, or your own homemade, recipe below)

1. Preheat the oven to 350F.
2. Grease a 1 1/2-quart casserole dish.
3. Add the cream of mushroom soup, milk, pepper and celery salt to the casserole dish; stir well.
4. Stir in the green beans and 3/4 cup of the fried onions. Note: The rest will be used as the topping.
5. Place the casserole in the oven and bake for 20 minutes.
6. Remove from the oven and top with the remaining fried onions.
7. Bake for a further 10 minutes, until the onions are lightly browned.
8. Remove the casserole from the oven and cool on a wire rack for 10 minutes before serving, to rest the dish and avoid anyone burning their mouths.

Serve hot.

Make and Freeze

This recipe will freeze well. Portion it out as part of your Thanksgiving TV dinners, or it is own container once it is cooled. Heat in the microwave, stirring occasionally, until warmed through.

14-Homemade French Fried Onions

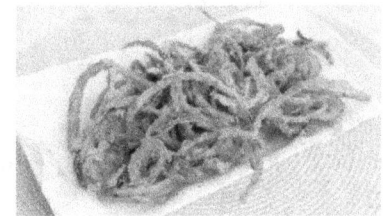

2 cups milk
3 large yellow onions, sliced into thin rings
1 1/2 cups all-purpose flour, or gluten free flour
1/2 cup corn meal
1 teaspoon of salt
1 teaspoon of pepper

oil for frying

1. Preheat the oven to 325F.
2. Line two baking trays with paper towels for draining the fried onion rings. Set aside.
3. In a large glass bowl, pour in the milk.
4. Add the onions, stirring them gently.

5. Soak the onions rings in the milk for 5 minutes.
6. While they are soaking, put the two flours into a large clean plastic bag.
7. Add the salt and pepper and shake the plastic bag well to combine.
8. In a sturdy deep skillet, heat up 2 inches of oil over a medium flame. Or, turn on your <u>deep fat fryer</u>.

Wash your hands well.

9. Remove a large handful of onion from the bowl of milk. Shake out excess liquid over the bowl.
10. Place the onion in the plastic bag and shake to coat.
11. Remove from the bag, shake off excess flour, and place the onions in the hot oil.
12. Move the onions around in the pan with a spatula to separate them out so they will fry evenly rather than in a clump. If you are using your deep fat fryer, spread them out in a single layer in the basket.
13. Fry until the onions look golden brown.
14. Remove from the hot oil and place on the prepared baking trays to drain.
15. Place the baking trays in the oven to keep the onions warm.
16. Repeat Steps 10 to 16 until all the onions have been fried.
17. Use the onions in your green bean casserole, or as a tasty snack any time without all the salt and preservatives of the store-bought kind.

Note: So the milk does not go to waste, use it as the base for any creamy soup, such as the cream of mushroom recipe above. The 2 cups of milk would make 4 batches of that soup. You can make the fried onions first, and then the soup.

Make and Freeze

Allow to cool fully. Store in an air-tight container. Use in any recipe that calls for this ingredient, or as a topping or snack.

Defrost for 15 minutes at room temperature.

15-Creamy Thanksgiving Mashed Potatoes

This mashed potato recipe certainly isn't low fat, but definitely delicious. In Evelyn's house, it's reserved for holidays only

This recipe serves 6. Multiply the quantities as needed.

6 to 8 medium russet potatoes, peeled and cut into chunks
dash salt
3 peeled cloves of garlic (optional)
1/2 stick unsalted butter, cut into pats
1/2 cup skim milk
3/4 cup low fat sour cream
3/4 cup plain 0% Greek style yogurt
Salt to taste
Black pepper to taste
Chopped fresh chives or sprigs of parsley (optional)

1. Place the potatoes into a large saucepan.
2. Cover the potatoes with water.
3. Stir in a dash of salt.
4. Add the garlic cloves if desired.

5. Turn on the flame to high.
6. Bring the water to a full rolling boil.
7. Lower the heat and cook over a medium flame for approximately 15 to 20 minutes, or until the potatoes are tender when pierced with a fork.
8. Drain the potatoes in a colander.

Discard the garlic cloves. Or, if your family likes garlic, chop finely and set aside.

9. Return the potatoes to the pan, or to your serving bowl.
10. Mash the potatoes with a masher.
11. Add the butter and allow it to melt.
12. Add the milk and mash the milk and butter into the potatoes just until you no longer feel any large chunks.
13. Using an electric mixer, with the motor running, whisk the potatoes and add the sour cream and yogurt a little at a time, alternating between the two, until the mashed potatoes are creamy but not soupy.
14. Add salt and pepper to taste and whip once more with the mixer. Beat in the chopped garlic if desired. Set aside the mixer.
15. Add parsley or chives as garnish.
16. Scrape out into a serving dish, or cover to keep hot and serve as is.

Note; For a richer taste without too much more cholesterol, add a tablespoon or two of olive oil.

Make and Freeze

Mashed potatoes do not generally freeze very well. If you wish to freeze portions, choose a waxy potato like a russet, not a powdery potato like an Idaho potato.

Candied Yams

4 large fresh yams, washed well
1 1/2 cup orange juice
Zest of one small orange (grated orange peel)
1/2 cup butter, frozen and cut into small cubes with a sharp knife
1 cup brown sugar
1 bag miniature marshmallows for topping if desired
Orange slices (optional for garnish if desired)

1. In a large pot of boiling water, boil the yams with their skin on until tender, about 40 minutes.
2. Drain into a colander.
3. Let the yams cool enough to be able to remove the skin without burning your fingers, about 15 minutes.
4. While you are waiting, grease an oven-proof casserole dish. Set aside.
5. Preheat the oven to 350F.
6. When the yams are cooler and peeled, cut each yam into about 8 pieces.
7. Lay them out in the casserole dish.
8. Pour the orange juice over the yams.

Sprinkle with the orange zest.

9. Sprinkle with the brown sugar.
10. Sprinkle the frozen butter pieces on top.
11. Place in the oven and bake for 20 minutes.
12. If you are adding the marshmallows, remove the yams from the oven. Spread the marshmallows evenly over the top, or in a pattern like stripes, and return to the oven.
13. Bake for another 10 to 15 minutes, until the yams are fully candied, or the marshmallows are puffed and melted, browned but not burned.
14. Remove from the oven and let cool on a wire rack for 30 minutes to make sure no one burns their mouths on the sugar or marshmallow.
15. Top with the orange slices for garnish if desired, and serve warm.

Variations

Pecans on top also add a nice crunch, but beware of the fat content in nuts and the fact that some people might be allergic. A handful of dried craisins will also add texture, taste and color. Add either or both instead of the marshmallows, or in addition to them, such as in stripes across the top.

Make and Freeze

This recipe will freeze well as part of your own homemade TV dinners. Allow to cool completely and drain any excessive liquid from the bottom of the casserole dish so the food does not become waterlogged when it freezes.

Yams or Sweet Potatoes?

A lot of people ask us what the difference is. The photos above show yams on the left and sweet potatoes on the right. However, in the USA, the truth is that they are the same.

Sweet potatoes and yams may look alike, but they are not related to each other.

The starchier yam comes from Africa and is related to the lily.

The sweet potato comes from the Americas and is related to the morning glory. Most of the 'yams' you see in the US are sweet potatoes.

It is believed the confusion came about due to African slaves seeing sweet potatoes in the US when they were brought here, and calling them yams.

In other countries, you might find both yams and sweet potatoes. In New Zealand, where Evelyn visits as often as she can, the tubers are a staple at the communal meals of the indigenous people there, the Maori, and known as kumara.

Kumara, pictured above, come in a number of varieties and colors, are much drier with a less sweet flavor than the American sweet potato. They are roasted in a pit for the hungi, or feast, and take on a wonderful smoky flavor from the wood used.

17-Roasted Root Vegetables

This recipe is super simple, but very colorful and festive-looking.

8 to 12 slender carrots, peeled and trimmed, and cut in half lengthwise
8 to 12 baby turnips, blanched, peeled and cut into wedges
1 or 2 large beets, blanched, peeled and cut into wedges
6 to 8 fingerling potatoes, scrubbed and cut lengthwise in halves
1 or 2 large parsnips, peeled, trimmed, and cut lengthwise in half or into quarters depending on how thick it is
1 or 2 medium onions, trimmed, peeled and halved, each 1/2 cut into quarters
1 or 2 fennel bulbs, peeled and cut into thick wedges

4 cloves garlic, peeled
2 sprigs fresh rosemary, or 2 teaspoons dried
1 sprig fresh thyme, or 2 teaspoons dried
Salt
Freshly ground black pepper
Extra-virgin olive oil

1. Preheat the oven to 400F.
2. Generously grease an ovenproof baking dish.
3. Put all the vegetables and herbs into the prepared baking dish. Season well with salt and black pepper.
4. Pour the olive oil over and toss to coat.
5. Place the baking dish in the preheated oven and cook, stirring the vegetables occasionally, until they are tender and golden brown, about 45 minutes.
6. Serve the vegetables in the casserole, which you should put on a hot plate or trivet on the table with a large serving spoon. Or transfer to a serving platter.

Make and Freeze

These vegetable will freeze well. Portion them out into your own Tv style dinners or freeze in a plastic container and heat in the microwave for 2 to 3 minutes until warmed through.

18-Rice Pilaf with Wild Rice

Wild rice can be quite expensive, but a little goes a long way.

3 1/2 cups low sodium vegetable broth
1/2 cup uncooked wild rice
1 tablespoon olive oil
1 large onion, chopped finely
2 large carrots, chopped finely
2 stalks celery, sliced finely
2 cloves garlic, minced finely
1 cup uncooked regular long-grain white rice
2 tablespoons chopped fresh parsley

1. In a large saucepan with a lid, place the broth and the wild rice.
2. Over a medium flame, bring to a boil.
3. Lower the temperature and let simmer for 25 minutes.
4. While the wild rice is simmering, cook the vegetables. In a large, non-stick skillet over a medium flame, heat the oil.
5. Add the carrots and celery. Cook, stirring occasionally, for 5 minutes.
6. Add the onion and cook for 5 more minutes, stirring occasionally.

7. Add the garlic; cook for 1 minute.
8. At the end of 25 minutes, stir in the white rice. Increase the heat and ring the pot to a boil again. Stir well.

Reduce the flame to low medium.

9. Stir in the vegetables.
10. Cover the pot and cook, stirring occasionally, for another 20 minutes, or until all of the liquid has been absorbed but the rice is still moist, and the wild rice is not too hard.
11. Stir in the chopped parsley.
12. Transfer to a warmed serving dish or casserole and cover until ready to eat.

Make and Freeze

This recipe will freeze well. Portion it out in your homemade frozen dinners, or place in a plastic freezer bag or plastic container. You can pack the bag flat in the freezer to save room. Thaw overnight, or heat nin the microwave for 2 minutes until heated through. Place in a bowl, fluff with a fork, and enjoy.

19-Down Home Flaky Biscuits

The secret to these biscuits is to handle the dough as little and possible and not keep rolling it and re-rolling it to cut out shapes.

3 cups all-purpose flour
1 tablespoon baking powder
1 1/2 teaspoons salt
1/4 pound (1 stick) cold unsalted butter, cubed
1 cup heavy cream
extra flour for dusting
3 tablespoons melted butter for brushing the tops

1-Preheat the oven to 325F.
2-Line a baking sheet with cooking parchment.
3-In a large glass bowl, sift together the flour, baking powder and salt.
4-Using a pastry cutter or two knives, cut the butter into the flour mixture until the butter pieces are the size of small peas.
5-Make a well in the center of the ingredients and add the cream.
6-Stir to moisten the ingredients.
7-Knead the ingredients by hand lightly until a rather shaggy

and floury dough starts to form.
8-Flour a piece of wax paper or a clean work surface.
9-Turn out the dough onto the floured work area.
10-Flour your hands and knead lightly until the dough is smooth and all of the ingredients have been incorporated. Do not overknead or be too heavy handed.
11-Pat out the dough so that it is about 1 inch thick, shaping the dough into a rough-looking rectangle or square.
12-Using a sharp knife, cut the shape into your desired number of portions, 8 to 12 pieces.
13-Place each biscuit on the baking sheet, about 1/2 inch apart. Cup them with your hands on either side and all around each biscuit if you want them to look more rounded.
14-Brush the tops with the melted butter.
15-Bake in the oven on the middle rack for 11 minutes.
16-Turn the pan around so the biscuits at the front now become the biscuits at the back and vice versa.
17-Bake for an additional 10 to 12 minutes, or until the biscuits are golden brown on top.
18-Remove from the oven and cool on the baking sheet for 10 minutes.
19-Place the biscuits on a wire rack to cool for another 10 minutes. Serve warm as a side dish for any meal.

Make and Freeze

Allow to cool completely before freezing if you have any leftovers. Thaw in the refrigerator and rewarm in the oven for about 5 to 7 minutes to serve them warm again.

20-Traditional Cranberry Sauce

This is actually a fun dish to make because the cranberries popping sounds a bit like popcorn.

1 cup sugar
1 cup water
1 12-ounce package fresh or frozen whole cranberries

In a large sturdy saucepan with a heavy bottom, boil the water.
1. Add the sugar and stir until dissolved.
2. Bring to a boil again.
3. Add the cranberries and bring the mixture back to a full rolling boil.
4. Reduce the flame to medium low and simmer gently, stirring occasionally, for 10 to 20 minutes depending on how thick you like it.
5. If you like your cranberry sauce whole, stir gently.
6. If you like it smoother, use the back of the spoon to crush some of the cranberries against the sides of the pot and stir well to combine.
7. Cover and cool completely at room temperature.
8. Refrigerate it until you are ready to serve the meal.

Safety note: NEVER try to lick the spoon or leave it within reach of children. The cranberries will be scalding when cooked.

Variations
Use 1 cup of orange juice instead of 1 cup of water.

If no one is allergic to nuts and you want more texture, stir in 1/2 to 1 cup of pecans about 30 minutes after you have turned off the heat under the cranberry sauce.

Make and Freeze
Place a spoonful in each of your own TV dinners. It does not generally freeze well because of the high water content. The liquid will separate out and stain everything red, so if you wish you can put it in the food container with the other items in a small piece of waxed paper to stop the run off.
If you want to freeze a container of it, allow to cool fully, place in a plastic container, and freeze. Allow to thaw in the refrigerator and either drain off the excess liquid, or stir well to combine once again.

21-Cranberry Pumpkin Bread

2 1/4 cups all-purpose flour
2 teaspoons baking powder
1/2 teaspoon salt

1 tablespoon pumpkin pie spice
1 cup brown sugar
1 (15 ounce) canned pumpkin puree, or your own homemade
2 eggs, lightly beaten
1/2 cup vegetable oil
1 cup fresh cranberries or dried craisins

1. Preheat the oven to 350F.
2. Lightly grease 2 a0 x 5 loaf pans, or line with foil.
3. In a large glass mixing bowl, sift together the flour, baking powder and salt.
4. Stir in the pumpkin pie spice and brown sugar.
5. In a separate, medium sized bowl, add the pumpkin. Stir in the eggs and oil.
6. Fold the pumpkin mixture into the flour mixture.
7. Add the cranberries or craisins and stir well to combine.
8. Divide the batter between the two loaf pans. Smooth out the top.

Bake side by side on the same shelf for 25 minutes.

9. Open the oven and turn the loaf pans so the front of the pans now goes to the back.
10. Continue baking for another 20 to 25 minutes, or until the loaves are golden and a toothpick inserted into the center comes out clean.
11. Remove the pans from the oven and cool on a wire rack for 10 minutes.
12. Run a knife along the edge of each pan to loosen the bread.
13. Then invert and cool the loaves on the wire rack for at least 30 minutes so no one burns their mouths.

Make Ahead and Freeze

You can make these loaves up to three months in advance. Allow to cool completely, wrap well, in foil and then a freezer bag. To defrost, thaw in the refrigerator the night before. They will make useful contributions to any holiday feast.

Or, slice and freeze individual pieces for a festive treat in any brown bag lunch.

22-Pumpkin Pecan Muffins

2	cups	all-purpose	flour
1	teaspoon	baking	soda
2	teaspoons	baking	powder
1	teaspoon		cinnamon
2/3	cup	brown	sugar
1	teaspoon	vanilla	extract
1	cup	pumpkin	puree
2	eggs,	lightly	beaten
1/2	cup	chopped	pecans

1. Preheat the oven to 350F.
2. Prepare a muffin tin with liners, such as festive Thanksgiving themed liners, or gold ones. Set aside.

3. In a large bowl, sift together the flour, baking soda and baking powder.
4. Stir in the brown sugar, cinnamon and salt. Mix well.
5. In a separate bowl, combine pumpkin puree, eggs and vanilla.
6. Add the pumpkin mixture to flour mixture until just combined. Do not over mix.
7. Fold in the chopped pecans.
8. Spoon batter into the prepared muffin tin, filling each cup about 2/3rds full.

Bake for 18 to 20 minutes, or until the muffins are golden and baked through.

9. Cool in the muffin tins for 5 minutes.
10. Invert the tin and tip the muffins out onto a wire rack to cool fully.

Note: If anyone is allergic to nuts, use raisins, golden raisins, craisins, dates, or prunes instead.

Make and Freeze

These will freeze well. Cool, place on a baking tray, freeze, then place in individual baggies. Place the baggies in a larger zippered freezer bag so you can take one out any time you need one. Thaw at room temperature for about 30 minutes, or heat in the microwave for 1 minute.

23-All Butter Pie Crust

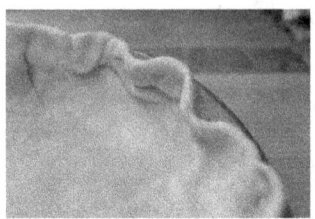

There are times when a ready-made pie crust will do, but Thanksgiving is special, so why not try making your own pie crust. It's not as difficult as you may think, and cheaper too

This recipe will work with the apple and the pumpkin pie recipes which follow, and with the tart recipe above. It makes one 9-inch pie crust. You can multiply the recipe and divide it into pie pans or tarts as needed.

- 1 1 1/2 cups all purpose flour
- 1 1/2 teaspoon salt
- 1 1/2 cup chilled butter cut into cubes
- 3 tablespoons cold water

Extra flour for dusting

1. Sift the flour and salt into a large glass bowl.
2. Add the butter cubes and cut them into the flour with a <u>pastry cutter</u> or two knives until the mixture resembles coarse bread crumbs.
3. or your fingers until mixture is well blended. Gradually add the water, 1 tablespoon at a time, mixing the dough gently after each addition. Once the dough has started to form, shape it into a large bowl.

4. Wrap the dough ball with plastic wrap or place in a plastic bag.
5. Place the wrapped dough in the refrigerator and chill for 30 minutes to an hour.
6. While you are waiting, prepare a clean flat surface to roil out the dough, such as a sheet of waxed paper.
7. Flour the waxed paper and your rolling pin.
8. When you are ready to roll out the dough, remove it from the fridge and unwrap it. Place it on the floured surface. Note: If you are making more than one crust at a time, divide the dough into the number of crusts you wish to make. Set the other pieces of dough aside.
9. Using your floured rolling pin, roll out the dough until it is large enough to cover the bottom and up the sides of a pie pan, a circle about 10 to 11 inches in diameter.
10. Line a 9 inch pie pan with the dough.
11. Repeat Steps 9 and 10 if you have made dough for more than one crust.

Lattice					Pie					Crust

If you wish to make a lattice pie, roll out a portion of the dough thinly and then cut into strips with a knife or lattice cutter.

Hint: To get the dough thin without sticking, flour the top of the dough. Place another piece of waxed paper on top and roll out until thin enough to make the number of strips you need to cover a pie. Remove the top piece of waxed paper. Cut the dough into strips, then peel off the waxed paper carefully to place on the pie.

Make			Ahead			and			Freeze

Refrigerate or freeze until you wish to fill it. If you are making more than one pie crust in advance, place a piece of waxed paper in between each one and place in a plastic bag to stay fresh. Bake from frozen. If you do not like a very dark crust when you are baking, always cover the crust edges with foil until the last 10 to 15 minutes of baking so nothing gets overdone or burnt.

If you have any remaining lattice pie strips, you can freeze them flat on a cookie sheet on the waxed paper, , then fold up and place in a plastic bag.

Prebaked Pie Crust

If you wish to prebake the pie crust, heat the oven to 325F. Weigh down the pie crust with some <u>pie weights</u> or bake as if if you want a fluffy crust. Bake the crust for 15 minutes. Remove the weights. Then the pie crust will be ready to be filled.

24-Easy Pumpkin Pie

1 pie crust (recipe above)

Pie Filling
2 cups pureed pumpkin (NOT pumpkin pie filling)
2 eggs, lightly beaten
1/2 teaspoon salt

1	1/4		cups		brown		sugar
1	12-ounce	can	low	fat	evaporated		milk
1			teaspoon				cinnamon
1			teaspoon				nutmeg
1 1/2			teaspoon				cinnamon
1/4		cup		butter,			melted

1. Preheat the oven to 350F.
2. In a large bowl, combine all the ingredients and mix well.
3. Pour the batter into the prepared pie crust.
4. Cover the pie crust edges with foil strips.
5. Bake the pie in the oven for 40 minutes.
6. Remove the foil strips.
7. Continue to bake for another 20 minutes, or until the pie is completely set in the middle.
8. Remove from the oven and cool on a wire rack for at least an hour to make sure no one burns their mouth with the hot fruit.

Make and Freeze

This pie will freeze well for up to three months. Freeze whole pies once they have cooled, or freeze slices in the pie pan. Place the pan in a plastic bag. Any time you need a slice, remove from the bag and microwave for a minute. Let sit for a minute, then eat and enjoy.

25-Homemade Creamy Whipped Topping

You can spread this over the top of the pumpkin pie and garnish with pecans or craisins as desired.to make the pie look a bit more dressed up and festive, or make a bowl of this and set it on the table when you serve dessert. It is fresh, without all the chemicals of the whipped toppings from the freezer and refrigerator sections of the grocery store. It is also lower in calories and does have some protein from the yogurt and cheese.

1/2 whipping cream
1 package low fat cream cheese
1/2 cup 0% plain Greek style yogurt
1 to 1 1/2 cups powdered sugar

1. In a medium sized glass bowl, using a hand mixer, beat the whipping cream until peaks start to form.
2. Add the cream cheese and beat until blended.
3. Add the yogurt.
4. With the mixer running, beat in the powdered sugar a little at a time, until it is fully blended and has reached your desired consistency and sweetness.
5. Use immediately.
6. Refrigerate or freeze any leftovers.

Make and Freeze

We freeze this in small plastic containers, and in plastic bags. The container can be put on the table any time anyone wants some whipped topping. Take out a spoonful and let it sit for a few minutes to defrost.

For decorating cakes, topping pancaked and so on, we defrost a plastic bag of the topping in the refrigerator overnight. Then we gather all of the topping into one corner of the bag. We snip the tip of the bag off and use it as an icing bag.

26-Fancy Lattice Apple Pie

1 all-butter pie crust with lattice strips (see recipe above)

Pie Filling
8 cups peeled and sliced granny smith apples (or other tart apples)
2 tablespoons all-purpose flour
1 cup white sugar
1 teaspoon cinnamon
1 1/2 teaspoon nutmeg
dash of salt

2	tablespoons	unsalted	butter
2	teaspoons	fresh lemon	juice

Pastry Wash
1	egg	yolk
1	tablespoon	water

1. Preheat the oven to 375F.
2. In a large glass bowl, combine the apple slices, sugar, flour, cinnamon, nutmeg, salt, butter and lemon juice. Stir well to coat the apple slices fully.
3. Place mixture into pie crust and smooth out to cover the entire base of the pie and form a reasonably flat surface.
4. Cover the edges of the crust with strips of foil.
5. Bake the pie in the oven for 20 minutes.
6. While the pie is baking, beat together the yolk and water. Set aside.
7. Remove the pie from the oven.
8. Remove the foil strips from the crust.
9. Arrange the lattice strips on top of the pie. We like to leave a nice open weave to avoid adding too many more calories, such as you would with a double crust pie.
10. When the pastry strips are in place as you would wish, using thumbs and index fingers, pinch down on the strips along the edges of the crust and the pie tin to crimp them closed.
11. Using a <u>pastry brush</u> or paper towel, cover the pastry strips and the edges of the pie with the egg yolk mixture. This will give the pie a nice golden look but without baking the pastry to the point of shoe leather.
12. Return the pie to the oven and bake for another 20 to 30 minutes, or until desired doneness. Test the apples with a fork through the lattice and down into the pie to make sure they are soft. Note-If the crust started getting too brown,

cover it with foil and test the apples again at 5 minute intervals until they are soft.
13. Remove the pie from the oven and cool on a wire rack for at least an hour so no one burns their mouth on the hot fruit.
14. Serve as is, or with ice cream or whipped topping (see recipe above).

Make and Freeze

This recipe can be made up to three months in advance. Freeze whole pies as your contributions to holiday festivities. Defrost in the refrigerator the night before.

Or slice the pie and freeze the slices in the pie tin. Place in a plastic bag and remove a slice any time you fancy a sweet treat. You can reheat it in the microwave for 1 minute to thaw.

Food Safety Note:
The egg wash is made with raw eggs. In our kitchens, we use one pastry brush for this purpose only. Either label it, or buy a range of brushes in different colors to use for different purposes. Be sure to wash your hands thoroughly when handling raw eggs like this.

27-No-Bake Cranberry Crisp Cookie Squares

This is a festive and fun cookie recipe that even the children can help with.

4 cups Chex™ rice cereal or Life™ cereal (cinnamon Life works well also), half crushed, and half broken up in to smaller pieces
1 cup craisins or dried cherries for a sweeter taste
1/2 cup unsalted sunflower seeds
1/3 cup cashew pieces
3/4 cup packed brown sugar
1/2 cup light corn syrup
1/4 cup crunchy peanut butter, if no one is allergic, or 1/4 cup semi-sweet chocolate chips
1 teaspoon pure vanilla extract

1. Prepare a large baking tray with cooking parchment or wax paper. Set aside.
2. In a medium glass bowl, combine the cereal, dried fruit of your choice, sunflower seeds, and cashew pieces.
3. In a large glass microwave-proof bowl, heat the brown sugar, corn syrup and peanut butter or chocolate chips for 30 seconds.
4. Stir the mixture well.
5. Heat for another 30 seconds.

6. Add the vanilla.
7. Stir the mixture well.
8. Heat the mixture for 1 more minute until it is heated through and all the chocolate is completely melted.

Add the cereal mixture and stir thoroughly until all the pieces are evenly coated.

9. Scrape out the mixture from the bowl onto the prepared baking sheet and spread it out to the corners of one side of the pan. Depending on how large the pan is and how thick you would like the cookies, press out to the opposite of the pan as needed.
10. Refrigerate the cookies for at least an hour, until chilled through and set.
11. Using a sharp knife, cut into squares and serve.
12. Any leftovers can be kept in the refrigerator in a plastic container for up to a week.

Yield

Makes about 2 to 4 dozen cookies depending on side and thickness. These will also make a great contribution to any party you go to.

Make and Freeze

These will freeze well and make a tasty contribution to any holiday meal. Allow to thaw for about 15 minutes before serving.

28-Spiced Oatmeal and Pear Cookies

With so many delicious foods in the fall, it can be easy to overlook the pear. But with all the trees she has in the family yard, Evelyn tries to come up with new ways to use their harvest every year. Here is one tasty yet elegant suggestion.

4 large pears such as Bosc or Bartlett, peeled, cored and quartered
2 teaspoons cinnamon
1/2 teaspoon nutmeg
1/4 cup butter
1 cup brown sugar, packed
1 teaspoon pure vanilla extract
2 eggs
1 cup all-purpose flour
1 teaspoons baking powder
1 teaspoons baking powder
dash salt
1 cup rolled oats
1/2 teaspoon ground ginger
1/4 cup crystalized ginger, chopped
3/4 cup semi-sweet or dark chocolate chips (or white chocolate chips for a more delicate cookie)

1. Preheat the oven to 350F.
2. Prepare 2 or 3 baking sheets by lining them with cooking parchment or Silpat.
3. In your food processor, using the sharp blade, process all of the pears until they are chopped finely.
4. Remove the blade and place half of the pears in a small bowl and the other half in a microwave-safe glass bowl.
5. Place the microwave safe-bowl in the microwave.

6. Cook the pears on high for 1 minute.
7. Stir the pears.
8. Cook on high for 1 minute.

Stir in the cinnamon and nutmeg.

9. Cook on high for 3 more minutes. Set in the refrigerator to chill for a few minutes while you continue with the recipe.
10. In a large bowl, using a hand mixer, cream together the butter and brown sugar until smooth.
11. Beat in the vanilla.
12. Remove the pears from the refrigerator and beat them into the mixture.
13. Add the eggs and beat in until just combined.
14. Set aside the mixer.
15. Using a sifter, sift the flour, salt, baking soda and baking powder into the butter mixture.
16. Add the ground ginger.
17. Stir the liquid ingredients up from the bottom and continue folding in the dry ingredients until they are all moistened.
18. Fold in the cold pears from the small bowl.
19. Fold in the crystallized ginger and chocolate chips and stir well to combine.
20. Drop the batter by teaspoonfuls onto the prepared cookie sheets. You may flatten them with the back of the spoon for a more regular shape.
21. Bake for 11 to 15 minutes, until they are browned and set. Do not let them get too dark.
22. Cool on the baking sheet for 5 minutes, then transfer to a wire rack to cool completely.
23. Serve warm, or store for up to 2 days in a plastic container in the refrigerator until ready to serve. Remove from the refrigerator about an hour before you are ready to eat them.

Make and Freeze

These will freeze well in a large zippered freezer bag. Grab a couple any time you want a sweet treat or a dessert for a healthy brown bag lunch.

29-Sparkling Cranberry Punch

64 ounces cranberry juice cocktail (look for 100% juice, not a sugary blend)
12 ounces pink lemonade
1 liter seltzer or lemon-lime soda
thin slices of lemon for garnish, if desiredIn a large punch bowl, combine all of the ingredients.

1. In a large punch bowl, combine all of the ingredients.

2. Garnish with the lemon slices, if desired.
3. Chill well.
4. Serve in small glasses, or allow the guests to help themselves from the punch bowl, using a ladle.

Variation
If you wish, freeze the pink lemonade as ice cubes to add to the punch bowl.

This recipe will also work well with orange juice, for a different taste. In this case, garnish with thin slices of orange instead.

Make and Freeze

You can make the punch a day ahead and cover. This recipe will not freeze well.

30-Mulled Apple Cider

Apple cider is always a special treat at this time of year. This recipe can make it even more special. Serve hot or cold.

2 quarts apple cider (look for pasteurized)
1/4 cup packed brown sugar
1/2 teaspoon whole allspice
1 teaspoon whole cloves
1 cinnamon stick
1/4 teaspoon salt
1 pinch ground nutmeg
1 large orange, washed well and cut into 8 wedges
Extra cinnamon sticks for garnish, if desired

1. In a large saucepan, heat the cider to boiling.
2. Stir in the brown sugar until dissolved.
3. Add the spices and stir well.
4. Add the orange wedges, squeezing each one to release some of the juice.

5. Bring to a full rolling boil again.
6. Lower the heat and simmer for 10 to 15 minutes, until all the flavors combine.
7. Stir well.
8. Using a funnel lined with a coffee filter or paper towel, strain the cider into a serving jug.

Cover and allow to cool for 30 minutes so no one burns their mouths on the hot fruit.

9. Serve in small cups or mugs.
10. Add a cinnamon stick to each serving, if desired.

Make and Freeze

This recipe will not freeze well.

It can be made a day ahead and taken out of the refrigerator to serve at room temperature.

Chapter 9: The Thanksgiving Holiday Does Not Mean You Have To Gain Weight

We all know that Thanksgiving is a great opportunity to relax and spend time with family and friends.

Many of us also unfortunately know it is a great way to pack on the pounds, which can also lead to stress. Especially if you have 'food issues', or can't resist temptation.

While Thanksgiving has become associated with stuffing ourselves, there ARE ways to help curb your eating and give yourself a positive start to the holiday season.

Here are some tips for cutting back this year, so you don't end up paying for the one holiday for weeks afterwards.

Not eating too much on Thanksgiving can actually start before the big day. The stress of making travel arrangements, buying supplies, and coordinating get-togethers can cause you to start eating more before Thanksgiving day even arrives.

Remember to take time to de-stress, relax, and take some time for yourself during the month of November.

This is also a good philosophy to keep through the rest of the holiday season as well. (And make sure you don't go to town on the Halloween candy at the end of October either!)

One simple way to keep from gaining weight at Thanksgiving is to make small meal changes and substitutions while cooking. This does NOT mean you need to go buy a tofurkey.

White meat turkey is a wonderful lean protein with only one gram of fat per ounce. Compare that with dark meat turkey, at 3 grams of fat per ounce.

If that doesn't sound like much, well, it would be fine if most of us only ate one ounce of meat, but the fact is, if we even ate only 4 ounces, that is the difference between 4 grams of fat and 12. If we had 8 ounces of meat, that would be he difference between 8 grams and a whopping 24 grams of fat.

In addition to smart choices and portion control, we can also substitute certain ingredients for more healthy ones. Try adding extra spices to your meals so you don't have to add much butter or gravy.

You can also substitute skim milk to desserts and low-sodium chicken broth to gravy and mashed potatoes to add flavor without all the fat. You can also try alternate cooking methods like not stuffing the bird, and letting the fat drip off the turkey, or steaming veggies, and not coating them in butter, in order to make the meal healthier.

Never skip lunch on Thanksgiving, even if you're eating early. If you're really hungry when you go to eat, you'll end up eating a lot more, even factoring in the extra lunch calories.

Just remember to eat a sensible lunch, and not overeat before the big meal. You can also cut your portions on fatty foods by adding a healthy option to the beginning of the meal, like a non-cream based soup, and a salad, both high in liquid and good at helping you feel full.

Many of us do pretty well when it comes to keeping our portions small at Thanksgiving, but depending on how many options there are at your meal, all those small choices can add up to a lot of calories.

Instead of taking a little of everything, pick the things you want the most to eat, and take a sensible portion of each of them. You'll eat fewer calories, and you'll probably feel more satisfied because you got to eat all of your favorite foods.

In addition to eating less during the big event, why not go for a walk or do another physical activity after the meal. This will help get your digestive system revved up to deal with the extra calories and burn them off faster.

Or, if the weather is not so great, try an active indoor game like charades so the whole family can join in and bond at the same time.

With a little planning and effort, and mindfulness when you eat, and about what you cook, you can keep your waistline slim this Thanksgiving holiday.

Chapter 10: Organizing Your Leftovers

After a big Thanksgiving meal, most people end up with quite a bit of extra turkey and side dishes. Planning ahead for this so that nothing goes to waste can be a great way to make the most of one day of cooking, for many meals.

The first task is to carve any remaining meat off the bones of your turkey carcass. Once you have it off the bone, you can portion it out into 3 or 4 ounces of turkey per serving, and stretch the food even further in a number of ways which we will discuss in a moment.

Once you get most of the meat off the bone, use the carcass for stock. Place it in a large pot with enough water to cover it, and boil it for an hour, until all the remaining meat can be scraped off the bone easily. Use this as the base for soup, stew, or turkey stock. Strain it through a coffee filter, package up some of it, and use the rest of it and the solids strained into the filter with some turkey and left over rice or egg noodles and vegetables such as peas and carrots to make your own delicious homemade turkey soup.

While your pot is boiling, organize the leftovers into make and freeze   meals.

<u>Three compartment microwaveable containers</u> give your family all of the fun and interest of TV dinners, but for far cheaper in terms of price per pound. Let your food cool, parcel it up and freeze. In this way, nothing will go to waste as your once fabulous Thanksgiving dinner that everyone loved ends up lost in the 'leftover shuffle'.

Use all of the leftovers you have first if they are suitable for freezing. Most of your meal should freeze just fine, with the exception of salads with leafy greens and dressing on them. It is always a good idea to serve the dressing on the side of any salad so it does not get all soggy, and so people who are weight-conscious can add their own as desired.

Nibbling on leftovers is fine, but here are some additional healthy ways to use that leftover turkey, so one day of eating excess does not turn into several days of stuffing yourself with stuffing.

First of all, if you are watching your weight, make sure you serve lots of veggies, and eat only the white meat.

Secondly, make sure, if you have guests over, to send the lion's share of the leftovers home with THEM, so you are not tempted to overeat for several more meals.

But, having said that, if you have cooked a sumptuous turkey breast, it is good lean protein you can enjoy. Here are some ideas:

Sandwiches

This is our family favorite. Simply slather mayonnaise on your favorite bread and add turkey. Enjoy! Of course, you can make this sandwich fancier by using toasted garlic bread, or adding some seasonings to the mayonnaise.

You can quickly whip up some gourmet style mayo by adding some of the packaged ranch dressing mix to it.

Instead of regular old sliced bread, make turkey sandwiches with fresh Italian bread, hogies, wraps, or ciabata bread for a different taste.

Open Faced Turkey Sandwich

Start with some really good toast. Rub a little garlic or butter on it if you'd like. Then, lay slices of turkey on it and cover with gravy.

Heat up some left over stuffing and stick it in the toaster oven or your regular oven to give it a nice little crust and dinner is ready.

Turkey and Rice Soup

If you cooked a whole turkey, use the leftover bones from the turkey and throw them in a large stock pot. Cover them with plenty of water and add some onion, celery, carrot and salt and pepper. Bring it to a boil and boil for about 45 min.

Strain out the liquid, return it to the pot, add some rice and leftover pieces of turkey. Add any vegetables you like as well and cook until the rice and veggies are tender. Then eat some, and freeze the rest-remember that the dark meat has 3 times more fat per ounce than white meat turkey.

Turkey Enchiladas

You can fix turkey enchiladas just like you would chicken enchiladas with your favorite sauce, tortillas and cheese. Just shred the white and dark meat turkey, (aiming for the white because it has 3 times less fat) and heat it with some cheese and enchilada sauce. Spoon the mixture on flour or corn tortillas and roll them up.

Place the tortilla rolls in a greased baking dish and top with more enchilada sauce and plenty of low-fat cheese. Then bake them up until the cheese is nice and bubbly. They are a great way to use turkey in something that has a completely different flavor.

We love the 75% reduced fat Cabot Sharp Cheddar, great flavor and works well in recipes, but with a lot less fat and calories.

Turkey Wraps

Tired of turkey sandwiches? Use a tortilla instead. Pile on lettuce, raw veggies and plenty of turkey. Top with some ranch dressing and roll it up for a portable lunch or snack.

Another fun idea is to mix shredded turkey with a little mayonnaise, some chopped apple, grapes and a few walnuts for a turkey salad wrap.

Again, keep in mind that the white meat has a lot less fat than the dark meat turkey.

Turkey Salad

You can make traditional turkey salad as you would chicken salad, but beware of the mayonnaise, which can pile on the calories to an otherwise not too fattening few slices of white meat turkey. Cube the turkey, add celery and a dash of tarragon, and some mayo and a few tablespoons of 0% Greek style plain yogurt. Serve on your favorite bread, or in a roll or wrap.

Tossed Salad with Turkey

Make a gorgeous, colorful salad, using all the vegetables you can find in your fridge and freezer. Add turkey medallions to the top and add your favorite salad dressing.

Turkey Caesar Salad

Make a turkey Caesar salad with romaine lettuce, turkey, shaved parmesan cheese, croutons and Caesar dressing.

Turkey Chili

Shred your leftover turkey and cook it along with beans, tomatoes and your favorite chili seasonings. Of course you can also toss in any leftover veggies like corn or green beans, and cook them right along with the rest of the chili ingredients. Serve with cornbread for a hearty treat.

Turkey Shepherd's Pie

Cut up the cooked turkey, add peas, carrots and corn, and top with any leftover mashed potatoes. For an interesting twist, mash any remaining yams and top it with them. You might wish to scrape off the marshmallows, if you added them, so the dish is not so sweet.

Turkey Hash

For example, if you are going to make turkey hash for 4 people, estimate anywhere from 12 to 16 ounces of turkey meat will be needed. Round out the dish with beans, tomatoes and corn, with tortillas, salsa and so on for a complete Mexican-style meal.

Turkey Stir Fry

For a stir fry for 8 people, you would need 32 ounces of meat, or 2 pounds. Round out the dish with a bag or two of stir fry vegetables (you can get a good frozen assortment). Also add any leftover peas, carrots, corn and green beans (not casseroled) that remain from the meal and rice, or some noodles, and a dash of soy sauce and chili sauce for a Asian themed meal. Make and freeze any remaining food for your own TV style dinners.

Turkey Tacos

Shredded the turkey with two forks, stir well with salsa, and serve with wrap or taco shells. Add shredded lettuce and some cheddar. This is a great way to use up some of the dark meat without packing on the fat.

Use any one or all of these leftover ideas to stretch your turkey as far as possible, to make the most of one day of cooking and a little bit of prep work.

No matter what your family tastes are, there should be something for everyone, and any leftovers can be parceled up for make and freeze meals. The main point is to not allow your turkey to hang around for too many day in the fridge. If you know your family tend not to like leftovers, (no man ever seems to!) just freeze the turkey meat on its own in 1/2 pound or 1 pound portions, and use it later in any one of these great recipes.

Be conscious of food-borne illness, and always make sure you keep track of any leftovers to make sure they are not too old before you eat them, especially if they are poultry or pork. Better to freeze your food right away and reheat it in the microwave, than for things to get lost in the leftover shuffle and thrown away, or worse still, someone getting sick from week-old food.

Conclusion

Thanksgiving is a wonderful holiday at a glorious time of year. It is a harvest festival that helps us give thanks for the bounty we can enjoy each autumn. It is also a reminder that a long winter is fast approaching, and with it the end of the year.

One year over, another soon to begin. What a perfect time to take stock and be grateful for all we have, our small accomplishments, as well as huge victories, and above all, the people we have to share them with.

Thanksgiving is one day in the year where family, friends and food all combine into a special festival rich in historical and even spiritual significance. It is not supposed to be a stressful time for anyone, but one of mellow relaxation and enjoyment.

This report has tried to make some suggestions for a stress-free Thanksgiving that you and your whole family will be able to all enjoy and never forget.

Try even just one of the ideas suggested, or two or more. The most important thing is to relax, stay unstressed, and spend quality time with each other, not be constantly on the go or slaving for hours over a hot stove.

And to take time to remember the true meaning of Thanksgiving, to be grateful for all we have. It is a day to spend with your family being grateful for each other, not for your plasma screen. Thanksgiving is a day to spend together, living, laughing and loving, not stressing.

Happy Thanksgiving and Blessings to all!

Part 2

Introduction

Welcome in the red and gold hues of the leaves on the trees, the crisp cold air, and the smoke wisps leaping out of chimneys. This marks the beginning of a most wonderful family season.

Autumn is for families and togetherness, and what better way to celebrate all of that than to give thanks for everything that you have. Thanksgiving provides a chance for you and your close ones to feast together, but most importantly to spend time together. And if this holiday is about spending time with those that you love, then the last thing you want to do is be stuck in the kitchen, sweating away, creating complicated dishes.

And that's why we've created 47 Easy Thanksgiving Meals You Can Make All Year Round.

Thanksgiving doesn't have to be complicated at all; in fact it can be quite easy, as easy as any Sunday dinner. It's just the perfectionist in you, and probably all those sitcoms that feature the inevitable Thanksgiving day disaster, that make you fear the holiday meal.

But no more! Never again are you going to worry about cooking a Thanksgiving dinner because we've created easy dishes that are delicious and simple, and will make you a kitchen hero!

The dishes featured in 47 Easy Thanksgiving Recipes You Can Make All Year Round are exactly that. They are perfect for your Thanksgiving table, but you can also use these recipes to make meals for your family throughout the year.

This book helps you create Thanksgiving classics like Turkey with simplicity. We've also got some non-traditional Thanksgiving mains like Orange Duck and Chicken and Cauliflower bonanza for you to try!

The recipes included in this book provide numerous options for a variety of diets ranging from Paleo to Vegetarian to Gluten-Free. There will be something for everyone at your table!

47 Easy Thanksgiving Recipes You Can Make All Year Round includes all sorts of yummy dessert recipes like super easy Crème Brûlée, Strawberry and Cream Layer Cake, and a recipe for truffles that's so simple you'll be gifting those little guys for years to come!

And when it comes to drinks, you are going to be rocking it! We've given you simple recipes for Fancy Schmancy Champagne Cocktails, Bailey's Coffee, and gorgeous Cinnamon Apple Smoothies that the kids will love.

Thanksgiving is about family and food, and has nothing to do with trying to recreate all those difficult 12-step dishes you see on television shows. The less time you're in the kitchen, the more time you'll be spending with your family.

The dishes included in this book are simple, delicious, and give you so many choices that you'll be using these recipes for all sorts of family get-togethers!

The important thing this fall is to make time and give thanks for those important to us. The delicious holiday food is just the plump cherry on top.

Wishing you a wonderful Thanksgiving!

From our family to yours.

Appetizers

Thanks For Cheese 'N Artichoke Dip

*Prep Time: 10 **minutes** minutes*
Serves: 5-6
Cooking Time: 20
Total Time: 30 minutes
Diet: Vegetarian

A hot cheesy appetizer is the perfect way to welcome your guests for a holiday meal. This particular baked dip, complete with a mound of artichoke hearts, has got all kinds of buttery flavor and gives a warm, fuzzy feeling inside. You can serve the dip with rustic bread, or crackers, or a bit of both if you'd like.

What You'll Need
2 cups aged cheddar cheese, grated
2 tbsp. cornstarch
2 cups evaporated milk
2 green onions
2 cups of artichoke hearts, chopped
Bowl

Saucepan
Casserole dish

Directions
1. Preheat your oven to 400 degrees.
2. Take the grated cheddar cheese and corn starch, and mix them in a bowl.
3. Then place the cheese, cornstarch, and evaporated milk in a saucepan over medium heat.
4. Continually stir as the cheese melts and a silky, creamy sauce forms.
5. Mix the chopped artichoke hearts into the sauce, and pour the mix into a casserole dish.
6. Place the dish in your oven for 10 minutes, or until it's browned on top.
7. Finally, sprinkle with green onions and serve!

Smoked Salmon With Dill And Cheese

Prep Time: 10 minutes minutes
Serves: 5-6

Cooking Time: 0
Total Time: 10 minutes
Diet: Gluten-free

Preparing a silky salmon appetizer is the perfect way to welcome your guests to a lovely evening. Not only is smoked salmon delicious but it is also supremely nutritious, which is especially great in these chilly months.

What You'll Need
1 lb. smoked salmon
¼ cup dill
½ lb. goat cheese
6 cornichons, finely chopped
½ tsp. salt
½ tsp. black pepper
2 lemons
Bowl

Directions
1. Remove the salmon from your refrigerator an hour before serving, in order to bring it to room temperature.
2. Combine the goat cheese, finely chopped cornichons, salt, and black pepper in a bowl, and mix.
3. Chop the dill and leave a few sprigs for garnish.
4. Now add the chopped dill to the goat cheese and mix them.
5. Lay slices of the smoked salmon flat, and spread them with the goat cheese.
6. Grab one of the corners of the salmon and simply roll it.
7. You can hold the roll together with a toothpick if necessary, although if the salmon is sliced thinly enough, you shouldn't have any problem.
8. Add the few sprigs of dill from earlier as garnish, as seen in the picture above.
9. Slice the lemons into wedges and place them on a platter.

10.   Serve it up!

Tomato Caprese Whimsy

Prep Time: 10 minutes
Cooking Time: 0 minutes
Total Time: 10 minutes
Serves: 5-6
Diet: Gluten-free, Vegetarian

This is the easiest fancy appetizer you're ever going to prepare! These Caprese bites are as easy to put together as crackers and cheese, but have a whole different element of style and elegance thanks to the use of juicy cherry tomatoes, mini Mozzarella balls and pesto. We've given these particular Caprese a whimsical treatment so they resemble mushrooms, but if you're feeling serious you can just thread a whole tomato and whole mini Mozza and leave out the sprinkling of cheese on top.

What You'll Need
20 Cherry Tomatoes
21 Mini Mozzarella Balls
2 tbsp. Pesto sauce
2 tbsp. Extra Virgin Olive Oil

20 toothpicks
Small paintbrush

Directions
1. Mix the pesto sauce and extra virgin olive oil, and set them aside for a moment.
2. Grate one Mozzarella ball so you have little snowflake like pieces for decoration.
3. Slice a tomato in half.
4. Now insert a toothpick through the center of the tomato and into the center of the Mozzarella ball.
5. Brush it with the pesto mix, and plate it.
6. Finally, sprinkle the tomato toppers with the grated Mozzarella.
7. Rinse and repeat!

Bacon-Wrapped Dates

Prep Time: 10 minutes *Cooking Time: 10 minutes*
minutes *Total Time: 20 minutes*
Serves: 6-8 *Diet: Gluten-free, Paleo*

This combination of sweet and salty is enough to turn anyone into a Paleo convert. In fact, you don't have to be eating Paleo to appreciate the beauty of this simple two-ingredient appetizer. Just one of these bacon-wrapped dates pack both a powerful flavor and protein punch that can become rather addictive, so much so that you may not have room for the main event.

What You'll Need
1 lb. bacon, thinly-sliced
30 Medjool Dates, pitted
Rimmed Baking Tray
Parchment Paper
6 Wooden Skewers

Directions
1. Take your wooden skewers and soak them in water while you prepare the rest of the dish.
2. If your bacon is frozen, let it thaw before starting.
3. Preheat your oven to 400 degrees.
4. Next, line a baking tray with parchment paper.
5. Now wrap each date with bacon, and place it on the baking tray.
6. Once you've wrapped all the dates with bacon, take the skewers out of the water they're soaking in, and pat them dry.
7. Insert the wooden skewers through the bacon-wrapped dates. We've chosen to put five dates on each skewer, but you can adjust them as you like.
8. Place the skewers on the baking tray, and place the baking tray in the oven.
9. Let them cook for five minutes, then turn the skewers, and let them cook for another five minutes.
10. Finally... enjoy!

Tomato Pancetta-Stuffed Mushrooms

Prep Time: 15 minutes *Cooking Time: 20 minutes*
minutes *Total Time: 35 minutes*
Serves: 5-6 *Diet: Gluten-free, Paleo*

There's something about being able to pick up a whole "dish" and pop it in your mouth. These tomato and pancetta-stuffed mushrooms are in fact a complete dish all stuffed inside an edible mushroom bowl. You can even make some of these without the pancetta if you want a vegetarian version, but add some garlic to boost the flavor.

What You'll Need
20 Cremini Mushrooms
1 yellow bell pepper
2 medium tomatoes
3 green onions

½ lb. of pancetta
Salt
Extra Virgin Olive Oil
Cilantro garnish (optional)
Baking Sheet

Directions
1. Preheat the oven to 350 degrees and coat a baking tray with olive oil.
2. Slice the pancetta into ½" (inch) bites.
3. Stem the mushrooms and place the caps aside.
4. Chop up the mushroom stems.
5. Heat 3 tablespoons of extra virgin olive oil in a skillet, add onions, and sauté for 1 minute.
6. Add the pancetta and sauté for a minute.
7. Add the mushroom stems, tomatoes, salt (to taste), and continue to sauté for 3 minutes.
8. Place the mushroom caps on a prepared baking sheet, and drizzle with oil.
9. Scoop the pancetta mixture into each cap.
10. _____Now bake in the oven for 20 minutes, garnish with cilantro if you'd like, and serve!

Bell Pepper Hummus

Prep Time: 5 minutes minutes
Serves: 5-6

Cooking Time: 0
Total Time: 5 minutes
Diet: Gluten-free, Paleo, Vegetarian

So everyone's got a scoop level. Some people scoop heavy on dips while others lightly swoosh in and out. But we're pretty sure this hummus is going to convert all of your guests into scoop Kings and Queens. The earthiness of chick peas paired with the sweetness of red bell pepper is a heavenly combination. And the use of garlic is the link that pulls those two guys together. Chick peas are a great vegetarian source of protein and a good source of fiber. They can also be very filling, so watch your scooping!

What You'll Need
2 cups cooked chickpeas (canned is ok)
1 red bell pepper, stemmed, seeded, quartered
2 tbsp. tahini

4 cloves of garlic
2 tbsp. extra virgin olive oil
1 lemon, juiced
½ tsp. cayenne pepper
½ tsp. salt
Food processor
Pita Bread

Directions
1. Place garlic in the food processor and mince.
2. Add the remaining ingredients and mix until smooth.
3. Serve with pita bread, which you can slice into triangles for ease of scoopability.

Bacon Chips

Prep Time: 10 minutes *Cooking Time: 10 minutes*
Serves: 5-6 *Total Time: 20 minutes*
  Diet: Gluten-free, Paleo

Your low-carbing guests are going to be thrilled that they'll have something besides celery to dip into your choice of dips. These bacon chips work particularly well with creamy and/or cheesy dips as they give the chip a nice coat. The serving size here is an estimate. If you know your guests are going to swoon for bacon chips you can double up the recipe.

What You'll Need
1 lb. bacon
2 rimmed baking sheets
Parchment paper

Directions
1. Preheat your oven to 400 degrees, and line two rimmed baking sheets with parchment paper.
2. Slice the bacon strips into thirds; you can just slice the whole stack of them at the same time.
3. Lay each individual piece on the baking sheets and bake until extra crispy. This depends on the thickness of your bacon and appliance, but will be approximately 12 minutes. Turn the bacon over halfway through.
4. Allow the bacon chips to cool.
5. Serve with your favorite dip (goes well with Cheesy Artichoke Dip recipe which is Gluten-free as well).

Spicy Shrimp Appies

Prep Time: 10 minutes
Cooking Time: 5 minutes
Total Time: 15 minutes
Serves: 5-6
Diet: Gluten-Free, Paleo

What You'll Need
20 jumbo shrimp, peeled, deveined
1 tsp. curry powder
1 tsp. salt
½ tsp. black pepper
Extra virgin olive oil
3 lemons
Skillet

Directions
1. First things first, make sure your shrimp is thawed before you start.
2. Whisk together the juice of one lemon with 3 tablespoons of extra virgin olive oil.

3. Mix in salt, black pepper, and curry powder.
4. Add cleaned shrimp, cover, and refrigerate for half an hour.
5. Heat 4 tablespoons of olive oil in skillet over medium-high heat.
6. Remove the shrimp from the marinade and place them in the skillet.
7. Cook for approximately 1 minute and 30 seconds per side (or until pink).
8. Slice the remaining lemons into wedges and place them on the serving platter with the shrimp.

Zucchini Fritter

Prep Time: 15 minutes   *Cooking Time: 6 minutes*
Total Time: 21 minutes
Serves: 5-6   *Diet: Gluten-free, Paleo, Vegetarian*

Once you've had zucchini fritters coddled by dill, you'll never want zucchini any other way. These zucchini fritters are the perfect fall warm-me-up before a big meal.

What you'll need

- 8 zucchinis, peeled and grated
- 2 medium eggs
- 4 cloves of garlic, peeled and minced
- 1 tbsp. coconut flour
- 1 tbsp. dill
- 1 tsp. salt
- ¾ tsp. black pepper
- Extra virgin olive oil
- Griddle
- Bowl
- Grater

Directions

1. Preheat your griddle to medium-high.
2. Using a dishcloth, squeeze liquid out of the zucchini.
3. In a separate bowl, whisk eggs, garlic, paprika, salt, and black pepper. Mix.
4. Add zucchini and mix.
5. Sprinkle in coconut flour while continuing to mix.
6. Drop 2 tbsp. of mixture on hot griddle, and press down with the back of a turner.
7. Cook each side for 3 minutes.

Cheesy Spinach-Stuffed Crepes

Prep Time: 20 minutes
Cooking Time: 25 minutes
Total Time: 45 minutes
Serves: 5-6
Diet: Gluten-free, Vegetarian

This recipe may take a tiny bit longer than the other appetizers in this book, but it's worth it for the praise and delight that will surely echo out of each bite. Spinach and cheese are designed to love each other. And in this cake we've stuffed this duo into a crepe made out of coconut flour, so it's low-carb and gluten-free.

What You'll Need
3 eggs
¾ cup coconut milk
½ cup water
¼ cup coconut flour
Pinch of salt
1 lb. fresh spinach, washed and chopped
1 large onion, sliced

1 cup Mozzarella cheese, grated
½ tsp. salt
Coconut oil
Skillet

Directions
1. For the filling, heat 2 tbsp. of coconut oil in skillet over medium heat.
2. Add onion and sauté for a minute.
3. Add spinach and sauté until wilted.
4. Remove from heat, add salt, and mix.
5. Add ½ cup of cheese, mix, and set aside.
6. For the crepes, whisk the eggs in a bowl, then mix in the coconut milk, water, and salt.
7. Gradually add coconut flour while continuing to mix.
8. Heat 3 tbsp. of coconut oil in the skillet over medium heat.
9. Pour ¼ cup of crepe mixture into the skillet, and cook each side for 2 minutes.
10. _____Once all the crepes are done, scoop approximately 3 tbsp. of the filling you created in each one, and add a tbsp. of Mozza on top.
11. _____Roll up the crepes, plate them, and savor!

Spiced Almond Nut Butter Dip

Prep Time: 5 minutes minutes
Cooking Time: 0
Total Time: 5 minutes
Serves: 5-6
Diet: Gluten-free (dip only), Vegetarian

So, traditionally appetizers tend to be savory, but can you really think of anything that sings fall like maple syrup, cinnamon and nutmeg. We've taken the trifecta of fall flavors and incorporated them into an almond butter dip.
Pro Tip: shortbread cookies make the perfect scooper for your sweet autumn dip!

What You'll Need
2 cups almonds
¼ cup maple syrup
½ tsp. cinnamon
½ tsp. nutmeg
½ cup crème fraiche
Shortbread cookies
Food processor

Directions
1. Place everything in the food processor and mix until smooth.
2. Ladle into ornate serving bowl and serve with your favorite shortbread cookie.
3. Are you becoming a pro or are these recipes getting easier?

Sides

Garlicky Swiss Chard

Prep Time: 10 minutes   *Cooking Time: 15 minutes*
Total Time: 25 minutes
Serves: 4   *Diet: Gluten-free, Vegetarian*

Swiss chard doesn't get much play on the everyday, but it makes for a great green side. Swiss chard is chock full of vitamins and minerals, and is a nice rustic compliment to any Thanksgiving table.

What You'll Need
1 lb. Swiss chard
5 cloves of garlic, minced
3 tbsp. Parmesan cheese
Extra virgin olive oil
Skillet

Directions
1. Remove the hard ends on your Swiss chard and wash each leaf thoroughly.
2. Chop up the Swiss chard, and place it to the side.
3. Heat 4 tbsp. of extra virgin olive oil in a skillet over medium heat, then add garlic and sauté for a minute.
4. Add spinach, sauté for five minutes, cover it, then turn the heat to low. Let it cook for 10 minutes, and if water remains, cook for a little longer.
5. Sprinkle your Parmesan on top of the Swiss chard before serving.

How To Carve A Turkey

Your Turkey sits there, ready, glistening with sweet juices, waiting for you to take the plunge into that first decadent bite.

Whoa, stop right there and take two steps back. Before you get to eat your masterpiece, you have to prepare it. And to prepare the bird, you're going to want to know a few things about how to cut the bird.

What's to know, you might think. Or on the flip side you might not want to know cause you're meeting someone else to do the pleasantries.
But you know what?

It's important how you carve your Turkey because it lets you control exactly how much Turkey you're going to get out of it. And after putting in all that hard work you're going to want to get as much out of it as you can.

So let's go.

Place your Turkey on a cutting board and untie the strings holding the legs together.

Now make a slit in the skin where the thigh is attached to the body.

Pull the leg back and insert your knife where the thigh bone meets the body.

Now push the leg back, and as you put pressure on your knife, separate the thigh bone from the Turkey.

Once the thigh and leg are removed, you can separate the thigh from the leg by separating them at the joint that connects the two. They should easily pull apart.

Next, separate the wings from the body by slicing into the turkey just above where the wing joins the Turkey. Slice into the body cutting through the body to below the wings. You should now be able to easily separate the wing from the body.

Now over to the breast.
Start your carve about a third of the way down the breast. Slice down until you hit the wing area and repeat until you have dozens of slices of succulent turkey breast.

Carving up your turkey this way will ensure that you get the most out of your hard work, and aren't wasting any of the Thanksgiving bird.

Happy   Carving!

How To Set

A Table

The candles are lit, the plates are sitting perfectly, and the utensils are lined up, waiting for their marching orders. That's Thanksgiving at your home this year.

A perfectly set table commands respect for it and for the food. You've worked to your best abilities to create a beautiful meal for your guests, and that meal deserves a beautiful table as its setting.

Setting a table that just makes sense and is also pretty to look at it is quite simple, because the design is logical. So let's get started!

The charger plate is the large plate you are going to place at each seat. This plate stays on the table until your entrée is brought out. The charger plate is also the plate that will be the undersetting for any of the other courses you may serve prior to the entrée. It is on this plate that all of the other, smaller, plates will sit as you go through courses.

Next to this plate are the utensils on both the left and right hand side. The utensils are placed in accordance to which utensil you will need first, and based upon that you will work from the outside in.

Let's start with the forks.
The forks are placed directly to the left of the plate. Typically, you will have a salad fork and a dinner fork. The salad fork will be placed to the left of the meal fork in most cases, unless you are going to serve your salad after your entrée. If you serve seafood first, then you will have a fish fork that goes on the outside of your salad fork or vice versa, again depending on which course you're serving first.

Now for the knives.
Similar to the dinner fork, the dinner knife will be placed directly to the right of your plate, with the cutting side facing the charger plate. Your next knife may be a fish knife, and so that should go to the right of the dinner knife with the cutting edge facing the dinner knife. Finally, on the far right goes your salad knife, if that's what you're serving first.

The Spoon

If you will have a course requiring the use of a spoon, this spoon will sit on the right hand side of your last knife.

Glasses

Your glasses must be placed on the right side of the charger above the knives. If you're using a variety of glasses, you can place the shorter ones in front of the longer ones. If you're pairing wines, or using a particular glass with a particular course, then you should ensure that the glass is removed from the table after it has been used.

Napkin

The napkin is typically placed on the charger plate, or on the left hand side of the forks.

Butter Plate

You may want to provide your guests a butter plate. If so, you will place the butter plate above the forks. The butter knife will sit on the plate.

Extras

There is a ton of ways to spruce up any table. One of the easiest is to add candles. You can also add flower arrangements to the table as well as placards. The best and most important thing you can do for your table is to use ironed table linens. This gives the whole presentation a sharp, clean touch.

www.ingramcontent.com/pod-product-compliance
Lightning Source LLC
Chambersburg PA
CBHW072011070526
44583CB00015B/1435